SYMBOLISM REVISITED

NOTES ON THE SYMPTOMATIC
THOUGHT PROCESS

EDGAR J. RIDLEY

Africa World Press, Inc.

P.O. Box 1892
Trenton, NJ 08607

P.O. Box 48
Asmara, ERITREA

Africa World Press, Inc.

P.O. Box 1892
Trenton, NJ 08607

P.O. Box 48
Asmara, ERITREA

Copyright © 2001 Edgar J. Ridley

First Printing 2001

Book design: Getahun Alemayehu
Cover design: Ashraful haque

Library of Congress Cataloging-in-Publication Data

Ridley, Edgar J.
  Symbolism revisited ; notes on the symptomatic thought process / Edgar
J. Ridley.
    p.cm.
  ISBN 0-86543-961-3 (hardcover) -- ISBN 0-86543-962-1 (pbk.)
  1. Symbolic interactionism. 2. Symbolism. I. Title.
  HM499 .R53 2001
  306.4--dc21
                                        2001003494

This book is dedicated to everyone with African ancestry

-- the whole human race.

TABLE OF CONTENTS

ACKNOWLEDGMENT

This book would not have been written without the love and support of my wife, Linda, who has assisted me from the very beginning with my research. I would like to express my gratitude to Nik Zainiah Nik Abdul Rahman of the National Productivity Corporation in Malaysia for making it possible for me to share my work with Malaysia. Also, without the encouragement and understanding of my publisher, Kassahun Checole, my projects on symbolism and the *Symptomatic Thought Process* would not have gotten off the ground. I bear final and sole responsibility for my conclusions.

FOREWORD

As an international management consultant, my emphasis has always been to solve problems that arise globally. That is primarily what international management consultants do: act as problem solvers on a global basis for their clients. As an African born in the United States, I've always been interested in the problems of Africa and its relation to the rest of the world. After years of research, it became apparent to me that the problems of the universe were tied to symbolism and its resulting mythology and superstition.

Researching global problems from a multidisciplinary aspect is a very useful way to come to an objective consensus of what dynamics shape the world. My research has led me to my first book, the first in a trilogy, titled *An African Answer: The Key to Global Productivity*, which was published in 1992. This present book, *Symbolism Revisited: Notes on the Symptomatic Thought Process*, is the second of the trilogy. The third and last book in my trilogy will be *The Symptomatic Thought Process: Changing the Structure of Civilization*.

It is universally accepted that symbolism started in Africa and produced a scenario where mythology was the basis for decision-making and human activity. This is uncontested. Additionally, it is becoming increasingly clear that mythology, which was created by symbolism, also has to be given a new look. Mythology has created the superstitions that have hindered human behavior and good mental health for centuries. An example is in Africa, where we have had internal warfare and a pathetic, if not absurd, dependency on Europeans and the West to solve our problems over against depending on ourselves as Africans to solve our own problems.

It has been stated in UNESCO's **General History of Africa** series that myth governed history and was at the same time responsible for justifying it. When people make decisions out of mythology, you have chaos, wars, and anarchy as we see taking place all over Africa. However, let me be clear: this dynamic is not only happening in Africa, but globally as well - for example, in Ireland with the Protestants and Catholics, and the conflicts in Eastern Europe.

I am often asked about the symbolism of countries outside of Africa, especially to the extent that those countries prosper economically. Different countries' economic success compared to other countries within the Western hemisphere really have no bearing. What should be looked at is the white world's continual dominance over the nonwhite world and why that has taken place. All we have to do is look at symbolism, mythology and superstition to figure out why.

Symbolism has affected cultures all over the world. It has caused indescribable harm. That is one of the reasons Secretary General Kofi Annan of the United Nations continually talks about the brutality and the viciousness that people are waging upon each other globally. Annan seems to be puzzled by this global state of affairs. These wars and this inhumanity towards man are due to a symbolic thought process. This includes the prevalent dynamic of racism. Racism is such a cancer that the United Nations Commission on Human Rights is dedicating an entire global conference to it. The only way to eradicate that behavior is to initiate a *Symptomatic Thought Process*.

It will be noticed by the reader that I emphasize the dynamics of symbolism and its resulting mythology, rituals and superstition. If I seem repetitious, it is because I want to underline the importance of the *Symptomatic Thought Process*. I want it to be clearly understood that the dynamic of the *Symptomatic Thought Process* must take place if we are to achieve any semblance of a just and healthy civilization.

This book will shed light on why we need to take a new look at symbolism and its effect on the whole of civilization.

CHAPTER ONE

INTRODUCTION

In my earlier book, *An African Answer: The Key to Global Productivity*, I laid the groundwork for a concept that radically rearranges the way we make decisions. The concept stated that symbolism, and the phenomena generated from symbolism, is the cause of all of the problems that face civilization today. The three events originating from symbols are mythology, superstition, and ritual. All have functioned in concert to cause unparalleled harm and destruction to civilization.

Carl Jung has given the best and most useful working definition of a symbol, and this allows us to understand its relationship to mythology, ritual, and superstition:

> A word or image is a symbol, when it implies something more than its obvious and immediate meaning. A symbol is anything that implies, in any way, something more than is obvious and immediate to the casual observer.[1]

The above is not only the definition of a symbol, but it also leads to the meaning of mythology, which is a conglomeration of symbols told in story form.

---

[1] Jung, Carl G., Ed., *Man and His Symbols*, Doubleday, a division of Bantam Doubleday Dell Publishing Group, Inc., New York (1964), p. 21.

What is called symbolic is not symbolic at all. The philosophical theologian, Paul Tillich, gives a clear statement of symbols and their relationship to signs and mythology:

> Symbols have one characteristic in common with signs. They point beyond themselves to something else. The red sign at the street corner points to the order to stop the movements of cars at certain intervals. Red lights and the stopping of cars have essentially no relation to each other, but, conventionally, they are united as long as a convention lasts. The same is true of letters and numbers and, partly, even words. They point beyond themselves to sounds and meanings. They are given special functions by convention within a nation or by international conventions, as does mathematical signs. Sometimes, such signs are called symbols, but this is unfortunate, since it makes the distinction between signs and symbols more difficult. Decisive is the fact that signs do not participate in the reality of that to which they point, while symbols do. Therefore, signs can be replaced for reasons of expediency or convention, while symbols cannot.
>
> This leads to the second characteristic of the symbol. It participates in that to which it points. The flag participates in the power and dignity for the nation for which it stands. Therefore, it cannot be replaced, except, after a historic catastrophe that changes the reality of the nation that it symbolizes.[2]

Tillich's assessment is correct. However, while symbols participate in that to which they point, they are *not a part* of that to which they point. A symbol cannot have the original ingredient, but is always a complete plastic entity -- a substitute. In other

---

[2] Tillich, Paul, *Symbols of Faith*, from **Religion From Tolstoy to Camus,** edited by Walter Kaufmann, Harper & Row, New York (1961) p. 383.

words, a symbol always lacks qualitative originality, but a natural sign can have the original ingredient from which it originated.

Wet streets are a sign that it has rained. A smell of smoke signifies the presence of fire. All examples here produced are natural signs. A natural sign is a part of a greater event or a complex condition and to an expert observer, it signifies the rest of the situation, of which it is a notable feature. It is a symptom of a state of affairs.[3]

There is a distinct, qualitative difference between a natural sign and a symbol. A natural sign is a symptom, and a symptom is always a part and has the original stuff to which it points. However, a symbol can never possess the original stuff to which it points because it is a substitute and has no originality.

Symbols and symbolic thought are not natural ingredients of the neurological process. Scholars led by Sigmund Freud and Carl Jung have emphasized the importance of symbolism and its effect on our daily lives. In fact, Jung's work and his emphasis on symbolism led to his professional separation from Freud.

The response to my first book, *An African Answer: The Key to Global Productivity,* compelled me to write a more expansive and detailed account of symbolism and mythology as played out not only in our daily lives but in civilization as a whole. My concept is provocative and revolutionary, with severe implications for rearranging our behavior and the way we make decisions.

The 19th-century Egyptologist Gerald Massey, in his six-volume work, *The Book of the Beginnings, Natural Genesis*, and *Ancient Egypt: The Light of the World* emphasized the unity of symbolism and mythology. Massey, who was largely a self-taught Egyptologist, set out to prove that mythology, derived from symbolism, was the creator of all religions. He wanted to

---

[3] Langer, Susanne, *Philosophy in a New Key: A Study in the Symbolism of Reason, Rite and Art*, Mentor Books, New York (1948), pp. 94-95.

show symbolism and mythology originated in Africa. Massey gave a very compelling argument for the fact that all religions stem from symbolism and mythology and, indeed, religion is a symbol system whose other side is a total mythological system that has been mistaken for the literal truth.

In his day, Massey's ideas and thoughts were rejected by academia because of his emphasis on the African origins of civilization. This rejection was caused by racism. In Massey's time, the home of man was still considered to be Asia. The scholarly majority did not entertain the thought of Africa as the home of man let alone the beginning of civilization. Eventually, Massey's anthropological concepts were later justified by the fossil findings of Louis Leakey and Donald Johansen. Also, with the added application of molecular biology, it has been scientifically proven that the first man and woman were Black and their home was in Africa, and these black Africans were the creators of the first civilization. Gerald Massey and his concepts were unequivocally proven to be correct.

Massey was aided by another scholar, Albert Churchward, a surgeon with an interest in Egyptology and anthropology. His books were **The Signs and Symbols of Primordial Man, The Origin and Evolution of the Human Race,** and **The Origin and Evolution of Religion**. After rigorous study, Churchward agreed with Massey's conclusions emphasizing the African origins of the human race and the mythological origins of all religions. Massey and Churchward were among the first early thinkers to emphasize symbolism and the important part it played in determining the outcome of civilization. These scholars and their works were purposely not publicized or taken seriously by traditional academia because of the fear that such information would be disseminated on a mass scale.

However, their emphasis on symbolism and mythology was taken up later by Freud, Jung, Joseph Campbell, Rollo May, and others. In fact, Jung dedicated his entire professional career to the study of symbolism and its effects on the human brain. His final book, **Man and His Symbols,** was devoted to symbols. Professional conflict erupted between Jung and Freud because

Jung wanted to stress a different way of interpreting symbolism and myth. Jung's position was joined by Joseph Campbell, former professor of literature at Sarah Lawrence College. (It should be understood that symbolism and mythology are synonymous and that you cannot have one without the other.) Campbell was very impressed with Jung's revelation of the implications of living a mythological existence, as opposed to living without a myth.

Most scholars of symbolism have stated that symbolism is as natural as breathing; and the ensuing mythology is not only natural, but it is what keeps humans civilized. Psychoanalyst Rollo May states that mythmaking is essential in gaining and maintaining mental health. "History is determined by its mythology." [4]

Modern-day scholars are emphasizing the importance of symbols and myths that vindicate the earlier concepts of Gerald Massey and Albert Churchward. My basic assumption is that all religions stem from symbolism, which means all religions are mythological.

Unfortunately, most people do not understand how symbolism is used to mythologize history, manipulate behavior, and set in motion a way of thinking that creates the phenomena of racism, greed, neurosis and other forms of mental illness. Although Jung and May both postulate the belief that mythological symbolism is essential for mental health and well-being, symbolism, through its mythological content, has caused the distortion of scientific facts and created a barbaric civilization. Instead of being a panacea for humanity's thrust into fulfillment, it is a plunge into despair, derangement, and frustration for the whole of civilization.

Nothing can be accomplished by thinking symbolically. Our decisions should not be made from mythological assumptions. For example, the intertribal conflict and warfare in eastern Europe and Africa derives from superstition and mythology that makes people act out their myths in destructive and violent ways. It is the acting out of the myth that causes the destruction that we see

---

[4] May, Rollo, *The Cry for Myth,* Dell Publishing, New York, 1991, p. 92.

in Bosnia and Rwanda. Religion, which stems from mythology, has been the culprit that has brought about outright barbarism.

The idea that we have to rearrange our thinking about issues that have affected our lives for so long is upsetting to most, to say the least. But as an international management consultant, it is imperative that I ask the deepest questions about issues that are extremely important to civilization as a whole. That is what consultants do -- ask questions and solve problems. The problems that I am most interested in solving are those considered the most sensitive and difficult to answer. I wanted to know, for instance, the root cause of the racial conflict that has engulfed us for so long. In most cases, these problems have now reached the point where they are considered the norm, and that, in itself, is very sick. Indeed, some people have a vested interest in keeping society racist, in constant conflict, and barbaric. The educational system has taught us to shy away from dealing with these problems. It is no coincidence that the information that is kept from the masses is knowledge that is almost always a corrective to distortion. That has been one of the main ingredients of mythology: mythology distorts the truth so that the truth cannot be known. That particular equation comes out as *symptoms = symbols = myths*.

The prevailing racism inhibits breakthroughs in science and technology that would benefit everyone. The exclusion of people based on race, gender and class makes it impossible for us to initiate the level of research necessary to combat the major terminal diseases of the world. Mythology created racism. Racism will always be a prominent part of civilization as long as mythology is a prominent part. Therefore, in order to remove racism, mythology must be removed.

A thoroughgoing, careful reading of history tells us that it is only when we are not able to face the realities of life that we tend to mythologize and distort anything and everything that we do not want to be true. Symbols produce myth, superstition, and ritual, and these elements cannot be allowed to stand if we are to progress as a people. Nothing makes sense when it is carried out from a mythological point of view and when it is acted out symbolically. This is the dividing line between civilization and barbarism. We have to make the choice to live either symbolically (which is to live a mythical existence) or to live symptomatically (which means to live in a state of ultimate reality). We must face issues as they really are in their ultimate state. We must stop mythologizing to avoid dealing with reality and truth in any given situation. Quite to the contrary of many psychologists and psychiatrists, mythologizing events and things is tantamount to the most severe cases of mental illness. If we lived in a society in which we tackled problems honestly, without the excess baggage of our phobias and neuroses, the mythologizing of events could be prevented.

Amos Wilson, in his book, *The Falsification of African Consciousness*, depicted mythology as "hallucination."[5] Wilson is one of the few psychologists who have recognized the pitfalls of mythology. He saw European mythology as a hallucination that is used to oppress peoples of color the world over. That is, the history that is prevalent in the minds of the majority of people is a racist history. We know that history to be mythological. The prevalent historical account is one of prejudice that derives from a symbol system that allows us to live in, and accept, a mythological history and world.

---

[5] Wilson, Amos, *The Falsification of African Consciousness*, Afrikan World Information Systems, New York, 1993, p. 23.

CHAPTER TWO

THE USES OF SYMBOLISM

Carl Jung states: "a word or image is symbolic when it implies something more than its obvious and immediate meaning"[1] That is the beginning of symbolism and mythology, and it shows the unity of symbol and myth. Civilization is being destroyed by symbols and myth. It hasn't helped that scholars have sanctioned symbols and myths as a natural part of our thought processes. The problems that we face in today's world will never be solved unless we eradicate symbols from our lives. Carl Jung's emphasis that symbols always stand for something more than their obvious and immediate meaning is the true dynamic of the symbol. Symbolism is always an addition to what is already present and that addition is always mythological. That is one of the reasons why symbols and myths are synonymous. One scholar notes that,

> "The ancient history of man is being meaningfully rediscovered today in the symbolic images and myths that have survived ancient man."[2]

Actually, the symbolic images and myths that survived ancient man distort the history of ancient man, and indeed, the history of civilization. Only when we evaluate the *symptoms* of ancient

---

[1] Jung, Carl, ibid., p. 20.

[2] Henderson, Joseph L., *Ancient Myths and Modern Man*, from **Man and His Symbols**, edited by Carl G. Jung, p 106.

history can we truly understand what occurred in early civilization.

To solve the problems of civilization, the death of symbolism must take place. Throughout history, symbolism has caused the downfall of peoples and civilizations. It is only through the elimination of symbolism and its resulting mythology, superstitions, and rituals that we will truly live in a civilized society rather than a barbaric one.

Symbolism was born in Africa. It was in Africa that myths were created. It was in Africa that symbols and mythology started and spread all over the world. Albert Churchward, in his books, *Signs and Symbols of Primordial Man,* stated:

> . . .the first or Paleolithic man was the Pygmy, who was evolved in Central Africa at the sources of the Nile, or Nile Valley, and that from here all originated and were carried throughout the world, and that the most primitive phase of Mythology is a mode of representing certain elemental powers by means of living types which were superhuman, like the natural phenomena. The foundations of mythology were laid in the pre-anthropomorphic shape of primitive representation. . . .The pygmy is the oldest and first man. With him, language originated, and the first sacred ceremonies.[3]

The Egyptologist Gerald Massey states in *Ancient Egypt*:

> The one sole race that can be traced among the aborigines all over the earth, above ground or below, is the dark race of a dwarf negrito type, and the only one possible motherland on earth for these preliminary people is Africa. No other country possesses the necessary background as a basis for human beginnings. And so closely were the facts of nature observed and registered by the Egyptians that the earliest divine men in their

---

[3]Churchward, Albert, *Signs and Symbols of Primordial Man,* George Allen & Co., Ltd., London (1913), p. 3.

mythology are portrayed as Pygmies. . . .Bes is a figure of Child-Horus in the likeness of a Negroid Pygmy. He comes capering into Egypt along with the Great Mother, Apt. . . .In reality, Bes-Horus is the earliest form of the Pygmy Ptah. In both the dwarfs is the type of man in his most primitive shape. . . . In this way the Egyptian wisdom registers the fact that the Pygmy was the earliest human figure known, and that this was brought into Egypt from the forests of Inner Africa and the record made in the mythology. In this mode of registering the natural fact the Egyptians trace their descent from the folk who were first in human form--that is, from the Pygmies.[4]

There is no doubt that symbolism began in Africa, the home of man, mythology, superstition and ritual. Symbolism began in Africa and spread all over the world. As I have to restate over and over again, when we talk about symbolism we're talking about mythology, superstition, and ritual. These entities all stem from symbolism. A careful reading of history, be it African, European, Asian, or world history, clearly shows that the great conflicts stem from man's inability to think without mythologizing. In other words, any decisions and relationships that evolve from a mythological base are symbolic. When we see the conflicts in Africa, Europe, Asia, and Latin America, it is clear that myths are the ingredient, and when those myths are applied day-to-day, they become ritual. This causes the destruction of communities, societies and civilizations.

It is easy to see how symbolism destroyed Africa, with its tribal wars and inability to become productive by taking advantage of its great natural resources. Symbolism and its mythology have caused Africans to be the most symbolic people on the face of this earth. Marimba Ani, in her book, *Yurugu*, states:

---

[4]Massey, Gerald, *Ancient Egypt: The Light of the World*, reprinted by Black Classic Press, Baltimore, MD, 1992, p. 250.

The African world-view, and the world-views of other people who are not of European origin, all appear to have certain themes in common. The universe to which they relate is sacred in origin, is organic, and is a true 'cosmos'. Human beings are part of the cosmos and, as such, relate intimately with other cosmic beings. Knowledge of the universe comes through relationship with it and through perception of spirit in matter. The universe is one; spheres are joined because of a single unifying force that pervades all being. Meaningful reality issues from this force. These world-views are 'reasonable' but not rationalistic: complex yet lived. They tend to be expressed through a logic of metaphor and complex symbolism.[5]

Marimba Ani states that Africans and other people of color tend to be very symbolic. That view is also shared by Frances Welsing in her book, *The Isis Papers*:

The use of symbols (including the interpretation of dreams) reach their highest development in African and Asian cultures, and was of major significance in these cultures dating back to the earliest time (prehistory), long before there was any European cultural development.[6]

Also, in my book, *An African Answer: The Key to Global Productivity*, I state that Africans are the most symbolic-behaving people in existence, and this symbolism is detrimental to them. Although there is agreement that African people are the most symbolic-behaving people in the universe, there have been questions on the reasons why. In UNESCO's first volume of *The General History of Africa* series, they state unequivocally that:

---

[5] Ani, Marimba, *Yurugu*, Africa World Press, Trenton, NJ, (1994) p. 29.

[6] Welsing, Frances Cress, M.D., *The Isis Papers*, Third World Press, Chicago (1991) p. 56.

Myth, mythological symbolism destroyed Africa. . .
The issue of race is not so much a biological
phenomenon as a social myth.[7]

The explanation of Dr. Richard King seems to be the most
plausible: Blacks, Africans, are the most symbolic due to their
high melanin content. [8]

There is an assumption in the intellectual community that
modern man has lost his symbol-making desirability; in other
words, modern man is not creating symbols and myths. Actually,
modern man does not understand the extent of his mythical
behavior. He is creating new symbols and myths as well as
operating under the old ones.

As Edward C. Whitmont expresses in his book, *The
Symbolic Quest,* "The whole of life can be seen as a symbolic
quest."[9] Albert Churchward states:

By going back to primitive man, the pygmy, we find
the first symbol we use. He believed in a supreme spirit
and propitiated elemental powers.[10]

James G. Fraser in *The Golden Bough* documented
instances throughout history of how symbol and myth resulted in
superstition. Fraser really shows how superstition affected
peoples' behavior and, ultimately, their decision-making. In *The
Golden Bough,* Fraser shows how Europe adopted symbols and
myths from Africa and used those same symbols and mythology
in superstition. Europeans are a symbolic people, although not as
symbolic or mythological as Africans, and Europe adopted

---

[7] Ki-Zerbo, J., Ed., *UNESCO, General History of Africa, Volume I – Methodology
and African Prehistory,* James Currey Publishers, California (1989), p. 102.

[8] King, Richard, M.D. (September, 1984) The Symbolism of the Crown in Ancient
Egypt. Conference on Nile Valley Civilizations, Atlanta.

[9] Whitmont, Edward C. *The Symbolic Quest,* Princeton University Press,
Princeton, NJ (1969) p. 136.

[10] Churchward, Albert, *Signs and Symbols of Primordial Man,* ibid., p. 450.

Africa's symbolism, mythology and rituals. This is contrary to what Marimba Ani and other scholars have stated.

Following are examples of mythology, superstition, and rituals in Fraser's **Golden Bough**:

> Amongst the Omaha Indians of North America, when the corn is withering for want of rain, the members of the sacred Buffalo Society fill a large vessel full with water and dance four times around it. One of them drinks some of the water and spirts it into the air, making a fine spray in imitation of a mist or drizzling rain. Then he upsets the vessel, spilling the water on the ground; whereupon the dancers fall down and drink up the water, getting mud all over their faces. Lastly, they spirt the water into the air, making a fine mist. This saves the corn. [11]

This is an example of how the Indians of North America performed their ritual to bring rain. Another example follows:

> When a Cambodian hunter has set his nets and taken nothing, he strips himself naked, goes somewhere off, then strolls up to the net as if he did not see it, lets himself be caught and cries, 'Hello, what's this? I'm afraid I'm caught.' And after that the net is sure to catch some game. [12]

These rituals are performed to supply a need. Here is another example:

> Amongst the Antaymours of Madagascar, the king is responsible for the growth of the crops and for every misfortune that befalls the people. In many places, the

---

[11] Fraser, James G., The **Golden Bough: The Roots of Religion and Folklore**, Avenel Books, New York (1981), p. 14.

[12] Ibid., p. 10.

king is punished if rain does not fall and the crops do not turn out well. Thus, in some parts of West Africa when prayers and offerings presented to the king have failed to procure rain, his subjects bind him with ropes and take him by force to the grave of his forefathers, that he may obtain from them the needed rain. It appears that the Scythians also, when food was scarce, put their king in bonds. The Banjars in West Africa ascribe to their king the power of causing rain or fine weather. So long as the weather is fine they load him with presents of grain and cattle. But if long drought or rain threatens to spoil the crops, they insult and beat him till the weather changes.[13]

We can inscribe all these rituals and mythologies with what is happening in Rwanda. The ethnic conflict in Rwanda is due to the same kind of mythological or symbolic behavior and ritual making. People in the Congo place calabashes of palm wine at the foot of certain trees for the trees to drink when they are thirsty. In India, shrubs and trees are formally married to each other to be idols.

Wherever, as in Japan and West Africa, it is supposed that the order of nature, and even the existence of the world, is bound up with the life of the king or priest, it is clear that he must be regarded by his subjects as a source both of infinite blessing and of infinite danger. On the one hand, the people have to thank him for the rain and sunshine which foster the fruits of the earth, for the wind would bring ships to their coasts, and even for the existence of the earth beneath their feet. But what he gives he can refuse; and so close is the dependence of nature on his person, so delicate the balance of the system of forces, whereof he is the centre, that the slightest irregularity on his part may set up a tremor which shall shake the earth to its

---

[13] Ibid., p. 46-47.

foundations. And if nature may be disturbed by the slightest involuntary act of the king, it is easy to conceive the convulsion, which his death might occasion.[14]

Mythology, superstition and ritualistic behavior have never been advantageous for mankind. They have caused unproductivity and the decline of civilization as a whole.

Fraser states:

> The custom of sacrificing children, especially the first born, is not peculiarly Semitic. In some tribes of New South Wales the first-born child of every woman was eaten by the tribe as part of a religious ceremony. The Indians of Florida sacrificed their first-born male children. Amongst the people of Senjero in Eastern Africa we are told that many families 'must offer up their first-born sons as sacrifices, because once upon a time, when summer and winter were jumbled together in a bad season, and the fruits of the earth would not ripen, the soothsayers enjoined it.
>
> ....The condemnation and pretended death by fire of the mock king in Egypt is probably a reminiscence of a real custom of burning him.[15]

We must remember that, as Diop stated, Ramses II was the ruler of a people who systematically massacred reddish-blondes as soon as they met them, even on the street; the latter were considered strange beings, unwholesome, omens of bad luck, and unfit to live.[16] Egyptians killed everyone they saw in sight with red hair and pale skin because they thought they were odd and bizarre. Fraser confirms this:

---

[14] Ibid., p. 114-115.

[15] Ibid., pp. 236-237.

[16]Diop, Cheikh Anta, *Civilization or Barbarism*, p. 67.

With regard to the ancient Egyptians, we have it on the authority of Manetho that they used to burn red-haired men and scatter their ashes with winnowing fans. That this custom was not, as might perhaps have been supposed, a mere way of wreaking their spite on foreigners rather than amongst the native Egyptians red-haired people would generally be found, appears from the fact that the oxen which were sacrificed had also to be red; a single black or white hair found on a beast would have disqualified it for the sacrifice. The red hair of the human victims was thus probably essential; the fact that they were generally foreigners was only accidental. If, as I conjecture, these human sacrifices were intended to promote the growth of the crops -- and the winnowing of their ashes seems to support this view -- red-haired victims were perhaps selected as best fitted to represent the spirit of golden grain." [17]

As I stated in *An African Answer*, another popular object of mythology was the fish. The fish was used not only in African mythology, but in the mythology of people all over the world. Fraser states, for example:

The Indians of Peru adored the fish that they caught in greatest abundance; for they said that the first fish that was made in the world above (for so they named Heaven) gave birth to all other fish of that species, and they took care to send them plenty of its children to sustain their tribe. For this reason, they worshipped sardines in one region, where they killed more of them than of any other fish; in others, the skate; in others, the dogfish; in others, the golden fish for its beauty; in others, the crawfish; in others, for want of larger gods, the crabs, where they had no other fish, or where they knew not how to catch and kill them. In short, they had

---

[17]Fraser, ibid. pp. 306-307.

whatever fish was most serviceable to them as their gods. The Ottawa Indians of Canada believed that the souls of dead fish passed into other bodies of fish, never burned fish bones, for fear of displeasing the soul of the fish, who would come no more to the nets. The Hurons also refrained from throwing fish bones into the fire, lest the souls of the fish should go and warn the other not to let themselves be caught, since the Hurons would burn their bones. Moreover, they had men who preached to the fish and persuaded them to come and be caught. A good preacher was much sought after, for they thought that the exhortations of a clever man had great effect in drawing the fish to the nets. In the Huron fishing village where the French missionary Sagard stayed, the preacher to the fish prided himself very much on his eloquence which was of a florid order. Every evening after supper, having seen that all the people were in their places and that a strict silence was observed, he preached to the fish. His text was that the Hurons did not burn fish bones. Then enlarging on his theme with extraordinary unction, he exhorted and conjured and invited and implored the fish to come and be caught and be of good courage and to fear nothing, for it was all to serve their friends who honoured them and did not burn their bones.

The disappearing of herring from the sea about Heligold in 1530 was attributed by the fishermen to the fact that two lads had whipped a freshly-caught herring and then flung it back into the sea. The natives of the Duke of York Island annually decorate a canoe with flowers and fern, ladening, or are supposed to lade it, with shell-money, and set it adrift to pay the fish for those they lose by being caught. It is especially necessary to treat the first fish caught with consideration in order to conciliate the rest of the fish, for their conduct may be supposed to be influenced by the reception given to the first of their kind which is taken. Accordingly, the

Maoris always put back into the sea the first fish caught, 'with a prayer that it may tempt other fish to come and be caught.'

Still more stringent are the precautions taken when the fish are the first of the season. On salmon rivers, when the fish begin to run up the stream in spring, they are received with much deference by tribes who, like the Indians of the Pacific Coast of North America, subsist largely upon a fish diet. In British Columbia the Indians used to go out to meet the first fish as they came up the river. They paid court to them, and would address them thus. 'You fish, you fish; you are all chiefs.'... Amongst the Thinket of Alaska the first halibut of the season is carefully handled, addressed as a chief, and a festival is given in his honour, after which the fishing goes on. In spring, when the winds blow soft from the south and the salmon begin to run up the Klamath River, the Karoks of California dance for salmon, to ensure a good catch. One of the Indians, called the Kayera or God-man, retires to the mountains and fasts for ten days. On his return the people flee, while he goes to the river, takes the first salmon of the catch, eats some of it, and with the rest, kindles the sacred fire in the sweating-house. 'No Indian may take a salmon before this dance is held, not for ten days after it, even if his families are starving.' The Karoks also believe that a fisherman will take a salmon if the poles of which his spearing-booth is made would gather on the riverside, where the salmon might have seen them. [18]

The following further exemplifies how different countries symbolize and use fish in their mythology:

    [In Eritrea] This African country may take its name from the Greek word for the Red Sea, which laps around

---

[18]Fraser, ibid, Volume II, pp. 118-121.

its long shoreline, but for several centuries the idea of eating anything that came out of these waters was Greek to most people who live here.

Even when drought ruined crops and decimated livestock, a complicated brew of religious taboos, cultural traditionalism, lack of refrigeration and poor cooking kept Eritreans convinced that seafood was inedible. The resulting famines took lives that the sea could have saved.

Religion also played a part. The Islamic half of the population worried about sea creatures that were too insect-like such as shrimp and gravefish, and also fish apparently without scales, such as tuna, which some readings of the Koran deemed off the menu for Muslims. For the Christians, meanwhile, fish eating is an extricable link with Lenten traditions or fasting and self-denial. Eating it becomes a penitence -- especially since hardly anyone knows how to cook it properly. Highlanders would boil it for hours, like camel meat, and be repelled by the boney, tough and tasteless result.

During the Italian colonial period, from around the turn of the century to the 1940s, a few Eritreans learned to fillet and deep fry. But while fish is cheap in Eritrea, running around a third a cost of meat per pound, cooking oil is such an expensive luxury that it wiped out any savings. So deep-frying fish made about as much sense as cooking baked beans in vintage Bordeaux. In addition, filleting, which wastes 60% of a fish's nutritional value, was a poor use of food in a country where many people are malnourished.

But [things are changing] if Eritrea's newly-independent government has its way. With the tenacity and sense of purpose that helped win a 30-year war of independence against Ethiopia, the former fighters now have declared war on Eritrea's eating habits. To promote fish eating, they have assembled a front that includes international big guns such as the United Nations' World

Food Program, and enlisted local talent, such as an Eritrean comedian who has developed a routine making fun of meat-eaters. Eritrea's answer to Julia Child is cooking fish on the airwaves, and fish is most definitely on the menu at state dinners and school lunches.

In fact, school children have become guinea pigs in a piece of social engineering. As a captive audience, they're being fed seafood that Eritreans find especially unpalatable, such as deep-fried fish and sardines. 'If you start with school children, maybe in ten years they get used to it,' Mr. Etoh explains.

There's a new modern fish market in the capital city, Asmara, and a refrigerated fish van that patrols the back streets, trawling for impulse buyers by playing songs extolling the delectability of fish. Fish-promoting slogans appeal to both the palate and the patriot: 'Eat Fish -- It's Good for Us and Good for Our Country."[19]

Researchers from the University of Washington show that the consumption of fish cuts sudden death by cardiac arrest by 50 per cent. The National Center for Health Statistics reports that "Sudden death claims an estimated 145,000 lives in each year." Eating one serving per week significantly cuts the risk of death by cardiac arrest.

---

[19] Brooks, Geraldine, Eritrea's Leaders Angle for Sea Change in Nation's Diet to Prove Fish Isn't Foul, *The Wall Street Journal*, 6/2/94.

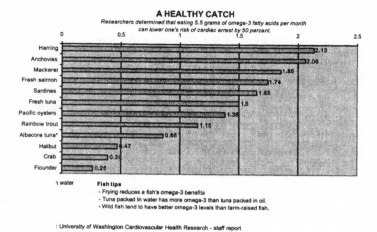

A HEALTHY CATCH
Researchers determined that eating 5.5 grams of omega-3 fatty acids per month
can lower one's risk of cardiac arrest by 50 percent.

Herring — 2.13
Anchovies — 2.06
Mackerel — 1.85
Fresh salmon — 1.74
Sardines — 1.65
Fresh tuna — 1.5
Pacific oysters — 1.35
Rainbow trout — 1.15
Albacore tuna* — 0.86
Halibut — 0.47
Crab — 0.35
Flounder — 0.26

n water   **Fish tips**
                - Frying reduces a fish's omega-3 benefits
                - Tuna packed in water has more omega-3 than tuna packed in oil.
                - Wild fish tend to have better omega-3 levels than farm-raised fish.

: University of Washington Cardiovascular Health Research - staff report

Diagram courtesy of University of Washington Library.

It is only by applying a *Symptomatic Thought Process* will we solve the problems that we face in today's civilization. Jung was wrong when he tried to emphasize the symbolic over the symptomatic. Freud was also incorrect. In fairness to Freud, he did not go far enough and didn't see the importance of a *Symptomatic Thought Process*. The main reason why people refrain from a *Symptomatic Thought Process* is because people do not want to face reality. Thinking symptomatically means the eradication of racism and of all phenomena that cause the destruction of civilization, as we know it. Psychoanalysts in the Jungian and Freudian camps emphasize that symptoms are made into symbols. I emphasize that the battle is whether to change a symptom into a symbol, to think symptomatically or think symbolically. Man has tried to make symptoms into symbols following the Jungian approach, but symptoms are not symbols. As I stated before in *The Neurological Misadventure of Primordial Man,* when man began to think symbolically it was a neurological misadventure.

Verena Kast, in her book *The Dynamics of Symbols: Fundamentals of Jungian Psychotherapy*, stresses repeatedly, "My intention was to make the symptom into a symbol." Therein lies the key to the destruction of civilization. George Ayittey, in his book, *Africa Betrayed,* documents how myths caused the destruction of African civilization, saying, "Much of this mythology was of deliberate manufacture to justify colonial rule."[20] Ayittey emphasizes how myths and the distortions of African leaders caused the downfall of Africa.

It is stated by scholars in various disciplines, especially analytical psychology, that it is only through a symbolic existence, as we live out our myths, which of course become ritual, that we can be whole and find our true self. Living that kind of existence causes mental illness, unproductivity, an inability to make decisions, and existential despair which is the reason for domestic and international chaos and violence. The whole of life is seen as a symbolic quest, and it is only as we eradicate that quest that we will have a civilization.

Eliade states, "'It seems that man is free to despise mythologies and theologies, but that will not prevent his continuing to feed upon decayed myths and degraded images.'"[21]
A large proportion of humanity does not realize that even when they decry mythology and symbolism and debunk myths per se, they continue to live mythologically by practicing racism and symbolic systems (such as religion) that continue to cause disruptions such as the ethnic conflict that we see around the world.

Edward Whitmont describes how mythology and images destroyed the life of Marilyn Monroe. He describes her suicide and its causes. Marilyn Monroe is but one celebrity, Grace Kelly is another, whose behavior was labeled by standard psychiatry and psychology as "misplaced symbolism". It is not misplaced symbolism that causes tragedy, it is symbolism, period, whether misplaced or otherwise.

---

[20] Ayittey, George B.N., *Africa Betrayed*, St. Martin's Press, New York, 1992, p. 17.

[21] Eliade, *Images and Symbols*, as quoted in Whitmont, Edward C., *The Symbolic Quest*, ibid., p. 80.

Black Africans created the first symbols, mythology, and rituals in the world. Those symbols and myths spread throughout the rest of the world, and were implemented eventually by all peoples of the world. Albert Churchward states:

> The human race therefore had its origin in Africa, and that by gradual development and evolution some of them settled in Upper Egypt and along the banks of the Nile, gaining here the first knowledge of Nature's Laws, and gradually acquiring a mythology -- later an Astral mythology -- and finally the perfected Eschatology.[22]
>
> The best educated Priests were as much attached to forms and traditional symbols as the people themselves, and they were most unwilling to give up any part of them; but the symbolism was misunderstood by the ignorant classes, and produced serious errors. The uneducated loved a plurality of gods, whilst the Priests and educated people, who could read and understand books, adopted the idea of ONE GOD, the creator of all beings in heaven and on earth. But when all is said against the Egyptian religion which can be said, the facts remain that it is not the religion itself, but the myths, wherewith generations of foolish Priests obscured their pure beliefs in monotheism and mortality, which existed in Egypt from the earliest times of the predynastic Egyptians.[23]

Churchward and Massey bear out the fact that Egyptian mythology was a religious system consisting of complex metaphors and symbolism that was very elitist. From the beginning, that symbol system caused untold harm and confusion for not only the so-called elitists themselves but the masses of people.

---

[22]Churchward, Albert, *Signs and Symbols of Primordial Man,* ibid., p. 241.

[23]Churchward, Albert, ibid., p. 403.

The symbol system in Egypt is universally understood to have been oppressive. Even in Robert Moss's novel, *Death Beam*, he states:

> ...the ancient Egyptian priesthood used language not as a means of communication, but as a way to establish and defend a monopoly of knowledge. Since common people couldn't read hieroglyphs, they stayed in their place.[24]

The symbol system in Egypt was the direct cause of the destruction of Egyptian civilization. It rendered a people helpless as it merged deeper and deeper into a mythological system that caused unparalleled unproductivity. Although Africans suffer the most from it, this same symbol system is affecting not only Africans but also people around the world. When white scholars approach African history, they implement an extreme system of mythology to distort it. Most white scholars from North America cannot tolerate the fact that Africa is indeed the mother of Western civilization. It is the genesis of Homo sapiens sapiens.

Africa was the first to produce civilization and Black Africans played the leading role. While Africans are the most symbolic people on earth, white people do practice symbolism, even if they would deny it. As seen by their religions and their racism, whites are deeply immersed in symbol and myth. Racism is ritualistic and mythological. White people not only practice mythology and are deeply symbolic but they will also be destroyed eventually by their symbol systems if they do not come to the realization that symbols must be eradicated in favor of a *Symptomatic Thought Process*.

There is a multiregional approach to human evolution that states that Homo sapiens evolved simultaneously in various parts of the globe and that Europeans are direct descendants of the Neanderthal. The theory, of course, rejects the concept that we are all recent products of our African ancestors.

---

[24]Moss, Robert, *Death Beam*, Berkley Publishing Group, New York, 1981, p. 118.

The work of Christopher Stringer, a researcher at the National History Museum in London, has reinforced the work of Cheikh Anta Diop and other African scholars on the origins of humanity. Dr. Stringer claims, in essence, that the whole human race is African. He uses molecular biology and other disciplines to prove that the concepts proposed by anthropologist and Egyptologist Diop are correct. Stringer's book, *An African Exodus: The Origins of Modern Humanity*, is a well-researched and honest attempt to show what truly occurred in African history. It exposes the *Bell Curve* and a multiregional approach as not only racist but scientifically absurd. Concepts like these can only come out of the mythological dreams of an ignorant populace.

My only qualm about Stringer's book is the continual refusal of practically all white scholars, no matter where they stand, to give credit to the scholarly and scientific work of African scholars. The book mentions Cheikh Anta Diop only once, casually, and ignores his great intellectual and scholarly contribution to world history. I can only conclude that there must be an innate fear and insecurity among whites about the intellect and forcefulness of African scholarship. It seems no matter what fence whites stand on, they still have that insecurity and fear of Black intellectual input.

I return to Marimba Ani's book, *Yurugu*. The following statement represents the standard so-called Afrocentric approach:

> The African worldview and the worldviews of other people who are not of European origin all appear to have certain themes in common. The universe to which they relate is sacred in origin, is organic, and is a true 'cosmos'. Human beings are part of the cosmos, and, as such, relate intimately with other cosmic beings. Knowledge of the universe comes through relationships with it and through perception of spirit in matter. The universe is one; spheres are joined because of a single, unifying force that pervades all being. Meaningful reality

issues from this force. These worldviews are reasonable but not rationalistic; complex yet lived. They tend to be expressed through a logic of metaphor and complex symbolism. . .rob the universe of its richness, deny the significance of the symbolic, simplify phenomena until it becomes mere object, and you have a knowable quantity. Here begins and ends the European epistemological mode.[25]

Ani is correct about the African worldview. Unfortunately, the present African worldview in terms of metaphor and symbolism is why we have a Rwanda. The present African worldview caused the destruction of African civilization. Additionally, Ani's statement about the Europeans and their lack of symbolism would deny the significance of the symbolic. Europeans adopted African symbolism and they used those symbols heavily in their religions and in their racism. Ani makes a critical mistake by de-emphasizing the role of symbolism in European culture. In *The Golden Bough,* Fraser illustrates repeatedly the symbolism and mythology that was prevalent in Europe.[26] That same mythology and symbolism had its origin in Africa. Amos Wilson stated that European history is mythology. He equated European mythology with European hallucination. Wilson went on to say, "Eurocentric history functions as mythology."[27] He also stated, "Mythology often can be seen as a form of denial of reality."[28] If we are to say that European mythology is hallucination, we must also be prepared to say African mythology is hallucination. This is not to deny the achievements of African history. This is to point out that mythology is bad no matter who is using it. Do not forget that European mythology is borrowed from African mythology.

The systems of symbols and mythology that African scholars would have us implement will never free African people.

---

[25] Ani, Marimba, ibid., p. 29.

[26] Fraser, James G., *The Golden Bough*, ibid.

[27] Wilson, Amos, ibid., p. 30.

[28] Wilson, Amos, ibid., p. 28.

Europeans used symbols to take over Africa and control African people. Europeans, and all whites, use symbols now to control the world. Marimba Ani couldn't get away from that, as she states in *Yurugu:*

> The images presented are almost the reverse of these distinctions. African and other primary societies are characterized as being "disordered," "uncontrolled," and "immoral." European society supposedly symbolized the movement away from this into order, morality and responsibility where the individual can feel safe. [29]

As we have stated before, the dynamic between substance and symbols is the key. We talked about the tendency to turn symptoms into symbols, which is synonymous with turning symptoms into mythology. The truth always wins out. That which is real eventually comes to the surface.

Marimba Ani discloses the possibility of two types of symbolism that are being used: one African and the other European. She states:

> Wade Nobles characterizes the African 'symbolic method' as involving a 'transformation-synchronistic-analogic modality', while the contemporary European cultural understanding of 'symbol' is as a 'representational-sequential-analytical mode.[30]

Nobles' characterization suggests that there are two symbol systems operable. There is only one symbol system, which was described by Diop in *Civilization or Barbarism,* when he stated:

> So let nobody tell us that Rameses II was White and reddish-blonde, for he was in fact the ruler of a people who systematically massacred reddish-blondes as soon

---

[29] Ani, Marimba, ibid., p. 269.

[30] Ani, Marimba, ibid., p. 207.

as they met them even on the street; the latter were considered strange beings, unwholesome, omens of bad luck, and unfit to live.[31]

The omens of bad luck that Diop talks about is of symbols being omens, and those omens of bad luck are mythology and superstition. The symbol system that brought about that phenomenon is surely the same symbol system that Europeans adopted and are applying to Africans in the diaspora.

There is one symbol system. That is completely compatible with Whitmont and his statement: "The whole of life can be seen as a symbolic quest."[32] In fact, the whole world tends to express itself through a logic of metaphor and complex symbolism. That's what makes the assertion of William Strickland so true:

> To maintain the myth of American righteousness, the government has no other recourse except to lie. Indeed, lying becomes the central political behavior of the state.[33]

Maintaining the myth at any cost is the primary concern of civilization. To maintain the myth, you have to maintain the symbolic process. It is only by eradicating that symbolic process can we begin to face reality and tell the truth again.

Marimba Ani states:

> Myths are a crucial aspect of self-determination and development. But they are culture-bound. African myths must explain to African people why and how we are a great people. When majority peoples accept the mythology of European progress, we are accepting a

---

[31] Diop, *Civilization or Barbarism,* ibid., p. 67.

[32] Whitmont, *The Symbolic Quest,* ibid., p. 136.

[33] Strickland, William, as quoted in Marimba Ani's *Yurugu,* ibid., p. 311.

system of myths and symbols that explain us negatively.[34]

Joseph Campbell also states repeatedly in all of his books how myths are critical for people to fulfill themselves and to gain a sense of what's really happening in the world. Campbell speaks of a mythology for Europeans. Since a portion of his mythological studies takes in the African mode of mythologizing, Campbell is also speaking of a mythology for Africans. Myths are not beneficial to Africans and myths have enabled Africans to be at the bottom of the world heap. What Ani and other Afrocentric scholars have to understand is that myths are not a crucial aspect of self-determination and development, but have enslaved Africans the world over. Also enslaved are the Europeans who have adopted the African myths by diffusion and other means.

One of the more regretful results of symbolism, mythology, and superstition is female genital mutilation. In her book *Warrior Marks,* Alice Walker clearly documents how symbol systems, as practiced through religion, enables Africans to manipulate other Africans in a most damaging way, causing the loss of lives of some African women. The devastating practice of female genital mutilation has been practiced intermittently in approximately 28 African countries. Rana Badri, a Sudanese activist with Equality Now, relays how symbol systems produce the behaviors that allow female genital mutilation to take place:

> "It's a very old tradition. Nobody knows where it originated from. It's like a symbolic thing. It's done for various reasons; some are religious. Some people mistakenly believe that it's an Islamic requirement. And other people, in other parts of Africa, perform it because it's a rite of passage into womanhood."[35]

---

[34]Ani, Marimba, *Yurugu,* ibid., p. 508.

[35] Rana Badri, as quoted by Harris, Shayla, in Secrets and Lies, the FADER, No. 6, Winter 2000, page 97/192.

As Badri stated, many Muslims believe that female circumcision is a religious necessity in order for a woman to be pure. Those women who reject circumcision are effectively ostracized from their communities: fathers disown their daughters, literally chasing them from the family home and/or village; men refuse marriage, since an uncircumscised woman is considered unclean; and in many cases, the mother of the uncircumscised woman is outcast also, as she is held responsible for the daughter's non-compliance. Although activist Badri is a Muslim, she recognizes the need to relinquish rituals as a means of liberating herself from the practice of female genital mutilation.

> "My family has done a lot of things. Because we are Muslims, we are expected to intermarry within the same family and cousins. But we didn't. We let go of a lot of rituals and a lot of ceremonies and other cultural practices......we took a completely different road."[36]

It is clear from Badri's statements that the symbol systems that produce mythology cause the behavior that allows female genital mutilation to take place. Hence, it is only by eradicating ritualistic behavior that we can eliminate the practice of female genital mutilation. This superstitious reasoning causes irreparable harm and death. It is extremely important to note that the dynamics of symbols and their resulting mythology are the cause. This is the problem with Africa and Africans. We continually use symbols to solve the problems that symbols create. Africa will never solve its problems unless we break out of this practice of behaving symbolically. We have to liberate ourselves from symbolism in order for our problems to be solved, so that we can participate in a civilization instead of barbarism.

A perfect dramatization of how symbolism destroyed Africa is in the film *Mark of the Hawk,* starring Sidney Poitier and Eartha Kitt. In that film, Sidney Poitier plays a revolutionary who

---

[36] Ibid.

has a relationship with a missionary who is trying to Christianize Africa. The missionary had just come over from China, where he tried to do the same with the Chinese. After failing and being expelled from China, the missionary goes to Africa. In the film, Sidney Poitier's character succumbs to the Christianity of the missionaries. Hence, Africa falls, while China continues to prosper.

If the whole of life can be seen as a symbolic quest, then the whole of life can be seen as a quest for barbarism. We can see that happening in Rwanda, Somalia and Eastern Europe. We can see it happening all over the world.

CHAPTER THREE

SYMBOLISM AND RACE

The statement in UNESCO's *General History of Africa* series tells quite succinctly what part myth plays in the dynamics of race and racism: "Race is not so much a biological phenomenon as a social myth."[1] Racism is a product of symbolism, mythology and superstition. Unless mythology is eradicated (and we know that mythology cannot be eradicated unless we eradicate symbolism), racism will continue to exist and flourish. Derrick Bell's statement that racism has become a permanent feature of American culture shows that some of us don't understand how to eradicate racism.

Racism is perpetuated by people who classify themselves as white. Their emphasis on keeping Black people oppressed shows they have a severe phobia of people of color. Many Black scholars such as Dr. Frances Cress Welsing and Dr. Richard King have critiqued the European preoccupation with, and fear of, people of color. Welsing believes whites have a fear of being a minority and that they are genetically inferior due to their inability to produce color. Welsing states that whites have a phobia about all people of color and fear genetic extinction.

King talks about the melanin that produces skin color and the fear of whites who are the offspring of Black Africans appearing some time around 20,000 B.C. as Cro-Magnon. Cheikh Anta Diop documents the environmental factors and different characteristics found in the southern and northern cradle. Diop confirms that white people, coming from a harsher environment, have different characteristics than Africans.

---

[1] Ki-Zerbo, J., Editor, *General History of Africa: Methodology and African Prehistory,* published by UNESCO, 1989, Vol. I, p. 102.

White people will somehow have to get over their phobias and fears and understand that racism is unproductive. Whites have to relinquish their symbols and myths in order to liberate themselves from their racism. Only then can advancement in various disciplines take place. Only then can we have a qualitatively productive and better world.

Racism and Eurocentricity are synonymous. A reading of history, if done symptomatically, easily illustrates the true role of Africa in world history. Africa was the cradle of civilization. Most of the technology in use today had its origin in Africa. All the religions and sciences had their origin in Africa.

Concepts about racism as espoused by Welsing, King, and other Black scholars have, for the most part, been ignored by whites. While these Black scholars have described the dynamics of racism very succinctly, the problem of its eradication has remained. Racism will only be eliminated by the complete expulsion of mythology vis-a-vis symbolism. Therefore, if man continues on his quest for a symbolic existence, racism will always exist.

The shooting of New York Police Officer Desmond Robinson shows once again the deadly effects of the symbolic thinking that causes myth. Officer Robinson was a Black plainclothes police officer who was shot by a fellow (white) officer who mistook him for a criminal suspect. Officer Robinson was a victim of symbolic thinking. When many whites see the color black or a Black individual, they automatically process "criminal" -- (bad guy) -- someone to be destroyed. The fact that Black and Hispanic police officers are at risk from their white colleagues shows how stereotyping and symbolizing creates a situation where a decision is based on myth instead of reality.

To prevent officers of color from being shot by white officers, a new method of training must be implemented that shows how symbolizing destroys the ability to think correctly. A *Symptomatic Thought Process* must replace a symbolic thought process. Then, one would not fall victim to mythological interpretations that are not based on reality. It bears emphasis - the only way that racism can be eradicated is to encourage people to experience a *Symptomatic Thought Process.* Automatically, prevailing symbolic thought processes and mythology would be erased. When one lives a mythical life, then reality can be interpreted and given any slant that feels comfortable and advantageous. However, by mythologizing, racism and its background are created. At the time of Officer Robinson's shooting, New York Police Commissioner Bratton stated that a special department panel would study the racial attitudes of police officers. However, if the study does not reach the core of the problem, which is to deal with symbolic images that affect our decision-making processes, nothing will be accomplished. Symbol systems as so broadly affirmed by scholars must be eliminated, because racism has its origins in mythology vis-à-vis symbols.

The case against symbolic thinking is heavy-laden with examples of people making decisions using mythological assumptions. We all cringed at the brutality inflicted upon Abner Louima, a Haitian immigrant, by New York police officers. No less, but fatal, was the violence meted out to Amadou Diallo, the young man shot 41 times by New York undercover police. This kind of barbaric behavior is due to symbolic thinking that results in overt racism. One gets the feeling that people will go to any lengths to control the behavior of the masses. The outcry against such torture, no matter who commits it, must be vociferous and lasting. These two examples show the myth of racism at work. Studies must be done to show the neurological impact that mythological symbols have on the brain. We must be courageous to insure that our research will not be tinted by personal agendas, and we must be objective in our findings.

Unfortunately, our major research institutions and universities have not been able to help forge scholars to deal with these issues. The academics within these institutions tend to exhibit some of the more severe symbolic behavior, and it is even more damaging because they are teaching students and perpetuating scholarship that is based on myth. A scholarship based on myth is a scholarship that had its origin in a system of mythological symbols.

The *Symptomatic Thought Process* is the only concept that can begin to address and eradicate racism. No other concept being practiced today has as its aim the elimination of all symbolism and mythology. I hope it does not take a bloodbath or complete race war to give people the initiative to deal with the cancer of racism.

By eliminating mythology, Blacks will learn how to be supportive of each other and make decisions void of myths, which will lead to unparalleled productivity. By adopting a *Symptomatic Thought Process,* whites will learn that the myths that they propagate and internalize about Africans and all people of color are false, and that they have nothing to fear from their minority status in the world. Whites will come to a full realization that they are indeed an African people, their ancestors were Africans, and as even European anthropologists have stated, we're all Africans underneath. Whites will realize that by perpetuating myths of denigration about people of color, they are really denigrating themselves, since their ancestors are Black Africans, and whites are the offspring of Black Africans. White people must accept these scientific facts. Instead, many whites continue to propagate falsehood and mislead the young so that they can have complete control educationally. One of the great tragedies is the educational system where there are two types of education: one white, that is full of misinformation and falsehood, and the other, Black, that is motivated by the truth as Blacks try to rid themselves of the yoke of racism-induced oppression.

Verena Kast, in her book, *The Dynamics of Symbols*, makes a good case for turning symptoms into symbols. That dynamic should be looked at as the phenomenon that caused the destruction of civilization. The dynamic between symptoms and symbols is the key to solving the problems that we deem unsolvable. Kast states, "My intention is to make the symptom into a symbol."[2] The symptom/symbol dynamic is the one that scholars should emphasize. It is the way our minds naturally

---

[2] Kast, Verena, *The Dynamics of Symbols: Fundamentals of Jungian Psychotherapy*, Fromm International, New York, 1992, p. 137.

work. Whitmont and Kast emphasize turning the symptom into a symbol, with Kast stating that the goal of therapy is to arrive at a symbol. Indeed, if we follow the thoughts of Jung, in many cases symptoms are symbols. However, if the goal of therapy is to arrive at a symbol, it is no wonder that people do not become healthy in therapy sessions or that the world is crazy and barbaric. This goal makes the whole world a myth. It makes the symbolic quest more urgent, therefore making problem solving impossible.

Kast gives us a paradigm of how she attempts to make a symptom into a symbol when describing a session with one of her patients:

> According to Jungian perspective, symptoms are also symbols; and these are the symbols that psychosomatics bring to therapy.
>
> If the goal of therapy is to arrive at a symbol and its linguistic formulation and interpretation through the symptom, it is basically because the physical symptom is a deeply unconscious expression of symbols and their formation.
>
> Even if we accept symptoms as symbols, it is recommended that we apply the same approach as with other symbols. The symptom must first be perceived emotionally, then we can continue with formation and interpretation.
>
> *An example and images for the formation of symbols in psychosomatic disturbances. –*
>
> During the course of therapy, a thirty-two-year-old man consulted his doctor concerning several functional complaints, and a general psychovegetative syndrome. His circulation was not satisfactory and he had pains in his lower abdomen. Since examinations revealed no somatic findings, he and I were to approach the symptoms through psycho-therapy. The analysand described his complaints very objectively.

In one session he reported that he had acute pains in his lower abdomen, a diffused, stabbing pain. He had cramps, too, and some diarrhea; but most uncomfortable was the mysterious, stabbing pain. First, I asked him if something special had occurred. I addressed the most important areas of his life. No, nothing special had happened. He was married and was very attached to his child. He had a good job and was an above average achiever. Neither in his family, nor in his relationships, nor at his place of work had anything special occurred. I gave him some crayons and asked him to draw his pain.

My intention was to make the symptom into a symbol by having him formulate it. Symptoms involving the lower abdomen are generally thought to be related to the ability to give, to elimination or to holding back and, in the extended sense, with separation processes. However, this is only a general indication, and rarely reflects the unique situation.

The analysand drew his first picture and said, "This is a green man on an obelisk." (Cf. color plate 18.) Then he fell silent. I wondered if at that moment he might have had a fantasy of grandeur. Sitting on an obelisk would mean he was high up, and enthroned above everything. I noticed the upper body was green and the lower body was barely present. There was no stomach to speak of, and no abdomen or genitals at all. The black wedge reached almost to the neck and seemed to impale him. He was no longer on the ground; he was enthroned. We looked at the picture for some time and exchanged our thoughts about it. Then the man said, "I'm incapable of functioning up here." This corresponded with the fact that he had drawn no hands or feet.

Of course, hands imply more than action alone; they are also organs of relationship. With our hands, we sense our relationship to others; we sense attraction, or repulsion. With our hands we express tenderness and can establish a very basic emotional contact. If we believe hands are no more than a symbol for action, we have become a victim to our ideology of do-ability.

The painter was unable to take hold of himself, nor was he likely to communicate his sense of contact. The choice of colors was interesting. We tend to associate the color green, a very dark green, with the calm of the forest, with vegetative life. This possibly indicated that he was afflicted in his vegetative system.

The black wedge moving up from the bottom was threatening. Black can be associated with night, dark, evil, or repression, and perhaps with beginning stages. Apparently, he was very actively and aggressively threatened--as the triangle indicates--by something that came out of the darkness, out of the night, out of the unconscious.

Black, he said, is the color of death. In other words, the pains in his lower abdomen were related to a fear of death. Fear of death is not only a fear of dying, it can also mean one is afraid to live. In any case, the drawing conveyed the idea that his pain had to do with the subject of life and death. Black can be the color of death; the goddesses of the underworld tend to appear in black.[3]

Kast's example shows that her patient was symbolic from the genesis. His sickness was a symbolic attitude, which is the problem of 95 per cent of the people on earth. The tendency to see Black as evil and/or death is certainly relevant to the racial problem. When one sees Black as death, we can see how that is readily applicable to the white, New York police officer that saw his fellow Black officer with a gun and shot him. Kast's example shows the destructiveness of thinking symbolically. How do we live our lives, symptomatically or symbolically? Nothing can be solved unless we deal with this issue. If we live out our lives symptomatically and symbolically, as Whitmont suggests, it is not only impossible but it is an entry into the genesis of mental illness.

---

[3] Kast, Verena, ibid., pp. 135-138.

We know that all religions are myth. In a very eloquent way, Whitmont describes the mythical experience and how it is synonymous with religion.

> The individual who works seriously with the products of the unconscious finds symbols and images arising within himself which have occurred over and over again in the religious experience of all peoples - whether within the framework of an organized religion or not. Since religion and a religious attitude arise spontaneously from the unconscious as mythological presentations, they are not, from the Jungian point of view, to be identified with any specific belief or doctrine, or for that matter with any teaching of conviction of the analyst. They are exclusively concerned with the individual's personal relation to ultimate reality. [4]

There is a continual quest to experience ultimate reality through mythology. This phenomenon has never happened, and will never happen, in human history. No experience with ultimate reality can occur through mythology via symbolism. That has been a thorn in the side of many theologians and philosophers: the continual expectation that an experience with ultimate reality can occur through symbols and the mythological experience. Psychoanalysts, theologians, and philosophers, and anyone proposing such a viewpoint, do an extreme disservice to mankind by proclaiming a method that can never be achieved or experienced. People becoming whole through a mythological experience vis-a-vis symbolism leads to the destruction of the human spirit and civilization. This is why racism is considered a permanent part of civilization. Racism exists because symbolism and mythology stop the perpetuators of racism from eradicating their racist behavior. Symbolism and mythology stop the victims of racism from liberating themselves and acting effectively and productively. One of the great errors is the assumption that

---

[4]Whitmont, *The Symbolic Quest*, ibid., p.84-85.

symbols can be used by therapists and psychoanalysts to work out complex problems. In actuality, symbols exacerbate problems rather than solve them. This is the reason why solutions are not available to society's most pressing problems.

Because racism springs from mythology vis-a-vis symbolism, it takes on a whole new meaning and context. Recognizing that racism is the product of a symbol system that expresses itself as mythology brings about a whole new understanding of the depth of racism and the damage it has caused to civilization. Because of racism, science has been unable to achieve its potential. Because Blacks and all other people of color around the world are being denied access to educational opportunities and jobs, the talent and knowledge that is available is not being used. There are many people of color who are in science and other areas who are not being listened to because of their color. Their ideas have either been excluded or distorted so much as to render them ineffective and irrelevant. The ideas presented by Blacks and all other people of color will never be used or taken seriously because they have been mythologized. This is pure racism, and this racism disallows the possibility of new discoveries. These new discoveries could solve the problems that we have today that are deemed unsolvable. Just think of the quality of life that we could have at our disposal if that mythologically based racism were not operable! That is one reason W. E. Deming wrote in his book, *Out of the Crisis:*

> With the storehouse of skills and knowledge contained in its millions of unemployed, and with the even more appalling underuse, misuse, and abuse of skills and knowledge in the army of employed people in all ranks in all industries, the United States may be today the most underdeveloped nation in the world.[5]

America's penchant for overt racism has denied Blacks equality in all areas of human life.

---

[5] Deming, W. Edwards, *Out of the Crisis*, Massachusetts Institute of Technology, Center for Advanced Engineering Study, Cambridge, MA, 1982, p. 6.

The history of mankind is being discovered by a symptomatic process. African participation in world history is becoming known symptomatically by discovering natural signs. Luca Cavalli-Sforza, in his book *The History and Geography of Human Genes,* leaves no doubt about the importance that genetics play throughout the history of mankind. Genetics and the evaluation of DNA are natural signs that are found in all humans. These natural signs become symptomatic as they are described. The findings of DNA are in agreement with the fossil findings by anthropologists.

Cheikh Anta Diop devised a method for quantifying the melanin content of the epidermis from dynastic Egyptian mummies. The preservation of the skin did not interfere with the detection of melanin. Diop demonstrated that the melanin content from the mummies was comparable to the quantity in the skin of present-day African populations. Diop's use and measurement of natural signs in the form of melanin revealed symptoms of the conditions of Egyptian mummies. This test that Diop performed is known as the melanin dosage test and it has been accepted by American science. But Diop, the multidisciplinary Senegalese scholar, was never taken seriously by the European and white academic community because he was a Black African. His work advances the understanding of civilization, but it was neglected by not only white scholars, but unfortunately by some of his own people in Africa.

Racism has its origins in symbolism. That symbolism, which developed into mythology, produced racism. If we accept the necessity of symbols and myths, then we accept the necessity of living in a world that will be in a permanent state of racism and racist behavior.

CHAPTER FOUR

SYMBOLISM AND BUSINESS: THE ECONOMICS OF MYTHOLOGY

There is an ongoing battle among consultants and consulting firms to see who can come up with the management concept that will be judged the leader of the pack to improve productivity. There is a huge market for quick-fix solutions to organizational problems.

Businesses are run by symbol systems. When corporations find themselves in a mess because of these symbol systems, they hire consultants to solve their problems. Consultants are viewed in today's marketplace as the ultimate symbolic analysts, to quote former U.S. Labor Secretary Robert Reich.[1] One of the things that re-engineering does is change metaphors. James Champy, former chairman of CSC Consulting Group in Cambridge, MA, stated that "today's managers must find new metaphors."[2] Tom Peters in his book, *Liberation Management*, devoted a chapter to "Finding New Metaphors." Finding metaphors is not the solution to business problems; it only enhances the problems that exist and creates an environment for new problems to flourish. Consultants who manipulate and change metaphors to solve problems are not effective. This is because they are, indeed, symbolic analysts who fail to see that they must eradicate the symbol systems. By eradicating the symbol systems, these

---

[1] Reich, Robert, Are Consultants Worth Their Weight? *Financial Times*, 1995 May 24.

[2] Champy, James, Breathless, And the Race is Hardly Begun, <u>AMA Management Review</u>, January 1995.

consultants would eradicate the mythological systems. This method only will solve the problems of corporations.

Once it is understood that we live in a mythological world, we see the consultant, as we discussed earlier, as one who is a master of symbolic manipulation. The consultant takes his skills of symbolic analysis into the business world and tries to solve problems. When mythology is seen as a denial of reality, it is readily understood why living in a mythological world is not only destructive but also self-defeating. Problems cannot be solved by engaging in the creation of new metaphors.

The idea that we live in a mythological world is hard to accept. One of the reasons it is hard to accept is because we base our decisions on a mythological framework. What that means is that most of the decisions that we make are wrong, incorrect, ineffective and non-productive. Remember: mythology is a denial of reality. If mythology is a denial of reality and we live in a mythological world, then our world is basically sick. The reason why racism is so prevalent is because we live in a sick world.

There is no doubt that the eradication of mythology would practically cure the mental illness and psychological problems that affect us in today's civilization. In today's business world, many people are on drugs such as Prozac and in psychiatric treatment simply because they are immersed in a mythological system with no way out. This is the prime reason why drugs used by executives are so prevalent in the business community, because manipulating metaphors and creating new mythologies creates a worsening of the psychological condition of the world population. That means the world business population is primarily mentally confused and psychologically impotent. Businesses cannot flourish if we rely on mythological answers to solve serious problems.

Amos Wilson stated:

> Whatever mythology we believe is one that organizes our approach to other people, our perception of ourselves and of other people. It provides answers. The answers

may not be right, they may be wrong; but it still provides an answer. And that's psychologically satisfying. Nothing threatens us and nothing upsets us like unanswered questions. Often Man projects a mythology in order to get himself out of his agony of dealing with unanswered questions and to put his mind at rest.[3]

If we have no answers to a problem, we supply a myth to satisfy our need for an answer. Consultants have no answer so they seek a mythological one. Corporations are paying out millions and millions of dollars to people who are supposed to provide answers but instead provide a myth!

One of the reasons why people still want that mythological answer is because they know that by getting rid of the myth they will get rid of a lot of assumptions they are holding and utilizing to maintain power and domination over other people. So, they are content to have mythological answers provided to them. Vincent Capranzano stated in an article in the *New York Times Book Review* called "Dancing With Myths": "Mythmakers, like their audience, like the commentators, are always trapped in their creations, and, I would stress, the delusions they produced."[4]

In the business world, Europe and North America's biggest nightmare is to see Asia and Africa doing business together. Malaysia is doing business in South Africa and hopes to use South Africa as a gateway to the rest of the continent. In fact, South Africa is Asia's biggest trading partner on the continent.

Assumptions held by whites are beginning to backfire. Their own mythological system is backfiring. Set-aside programs for businesses that are owned and operated by women and so-called minorities have undergone scrutiny and evaluation recently. The prevailing attitude among the white population is that the set-aside programs, geared to help so-called minorities, must be eliminated because racism no longer exists. Many whites perceive that the

---

[3] Wilson, Amos, ibid., p. 30-31.

[4] Capranzano, Vincent, "Dancing With Myths," *New York Times Book Review*, date unknown.

programs that are geared to help people of color and women have tendencies to produce reverse discrimination. This all comes out of a fear that whites have that they are beginning to lose their power. Whites are coming to a realization of themselves as being the minorities on the world stage. Whites have risen to a state of panic while still practicing racism to the highest degree. At the same time, whites insist that racism is at such a low that the programs that have been operating to give minorities an opportunity should be eliminated.

The Malaysian Prime Minister, Mahathir Mohamad, has a long history of pride in his country's achievements. Prime Minister Mahathir continually stresses the arrogance of Europe and the West, and he is very courageous in standing up to them. In an interview on *CNN International,* I stressed that although Malaysia has problems with its own mythological situation -- that is -- religious and ethnic conflicts just like everywhere else in the world -- they are making a concentrated effort to unify their country and join with the rest of the non-white world to produce a power base.

A symptomatic approach as opposed to a symbolic one would be to change the affirmative action plan geared toward bringing the ethnic Malay majority parity with the minority Chinese ethnic group. It has been suggested that a better affirmative action policy would be one that is based on economic need (instead of ethnic status) to help poor Indians and Chinese as well. This symptomatic approach would address the core economic need and could lead to a more unified nation instead of one where people identify foremost with their ethnic group. It would help turn the tide of racial violence and aid in the overall productivity of Malaysia.

It must be clearly understood that there are two powerful forces deriving from symbolism that affect global business. These two phenomena are racism and religion. With the rather recent emphasis on global transactions, we need a new sophistication in order to do international business. It requires a knowledge base that was previously thought unnecessary. The behavioral sciences have not done an adequate job in educating the workforce on how to do world-class business. The education of managers and the rest of the workforce in an adequate and unbiased way is not in the vested interest of those who would rather see the present way of doing business remain status quo. This produces an elitist, racist, and sexist system that continues to dehumanize the poor, reward the rich, and utilize technology for greed.

The behavioral sciences, as taught in our business schools, stay away from issues they deem touchy, sensitive, or uncomfortable. Business is successfully done by exhibiting appropriate behavior patterns. How one makes decisions is crucial to the outcome of any business transaction. The fad theories that are promoted by so-called motivational speakers and management gurus tend not to irritate or create a climate of deep thought, but are always on a very superficial level that requires no abstract insight.

By using myths as an escape for reality, we promote myths as the ultimate reality. This is why Tom Peters' book, *Crazy Times Call for Crazy Organizations,* or any management theory promoted in a book, will easily make the New York Times' bestseller list as long as the book is written by a white person. Non-whites are not supposed to produce theories or offer solutions that would affect the balance of power in the world. Despite the growing tendencies of whites to discount the factor of race and its influence in the business world, racism in today's world is more vicious and insidious than ever before. If this racism is allowed to stand, the result will destroy the world economy and any chance for progress in health, education, politics, business and the overall welfare. It will cause a continued rise in poverty. The tree is known by the fruit it bears. What is so disturbing about this racism is its total and unequivocal rejection of ideas of blacks and other people of color.

New concepts and theories by people of color can have an enormous effect on the enhancement of disciplines such as medicine, physics, science, and other major fields of study. The contributions of Africa and Asia are no secret. However, most concepts and ideas are tainted and discounted for the sole reason that their creators are non-whites. This practice must be eliminated so we can do business in an effective and efficient manner. This form of intellectual racism is supported and reinforced by academia, media, government, religion, business, and all areas where decisions are made to affect world policy. What is so appalling is the gall of whites and their mindless support of these racist practices.

In a global business world, it is neither polite nor considered appropriate to discuss racism and its continuous and damaging effects. It is not politically correct or good business practice to do this. The only code word that is acceptable in the global business community is diversity. This term has become an acceptable password for entertaining the ideas, out of necessity, of non-white workers in the global economy. What does diversity really mean? People of color and women are dealt with on defined terms. This limits the extent of business dealings. However, since whites are a minority, it will become next to impossible to keep the global majority, which are people of color, out of the workforce and other managerial positions as well. There is panic among whites to contain the effectiveness of all people of color. Whites, for the most part, may not verbalize this position. Their positions are presented in code words in daily business transactions. This sophisticated racism must be addressed no matter how uncomfortable it is. We can never have the attitude that racism is acceptable or here to stay. The only way to eradicate racism is to eliminate the symbol systems that cause it. Symbol systems produce the mythology that results in racism.

It is time to stop writing about racism and start offering solutions that will eradicate it. We have a solution that will eliminate racism and its resulting effects. This solution is beneficial to all parties involved. This is the solution: the elimination of all symbol systems. By doing this, we eliminate all of the mythological systems that create and support racism.

This concept offers a glimmer of hope to the statements in Derrick Bell's book, *Faces at the Bottom of the Well.*[5] Bell concluded that racism is a permanent part of American society. Any attempt to accept racism as a permanent part of society is insanely detrimental to the business community and the world at large. The business community must be willing and ready to accept new concepts that will challenge them to respond and think on new levels. The business community must stop overlooking the problems and start implementing solutions that will increase productivity.

As mentioned, the second most prominent phenomenon created by mythology is religion, a very sensitive topic. It is increasingly apparent that people make decisions based on their theological and religious belief systems and practices. When business people evaluate situations all over the world, invariably they come upon troubled areas where religion dictated the turmoil and unrest. However, in Africa, Asia, Latin America, and Europe, religion is still very personal. Any businessperson doing business globally will have to understand the importance religion plays in the decision-making processes of the people he or she is doing business with. A severe injustice would be perpetuated if we did not deal with the ramifications of the theological belief of the masses around the globe.

First, it must be understood that religion has its origin in, and was created out of, mythology. Conservative theologians and philosophers might have a problem with that assertion. In *Love's Body,* Norman Brown states that symbolism produced the myths that created all of the religions that are in use in today's world.[6] There have been countless debates about the impact symbols and myths have had on religion, with the understanding that myths have created all religion. There is no religion that did not manifest from mythology, directly or indirectly. Many lives have been lost in the name of religion. Much unnecessary bloodshed has take

---

[5] Bell, Derrick, *Faces at the Bottom of the Well: The Permanence of Racism*, BasicBooks (1992).

[6] Brown, Norman O., *Love's Body*, University of California Press (1966).

place because of this religious mythological phenomenon. In today's time, we can look at the situations in Ireland, India, Russia, and the Middle East. Traditionally, it has been viewed as inappropriate and bad manners to discuss religious beliefs. But it is essential to understand the religion and culture of the people you are doing business with. Many business deals have been based on that. The understanding of one's religious practice could mean the success or failure of a business transaction. It is becoming more apparent that one's mythological belief dictates and controls not only business decisions but life and death decisions as well. This shows the overwhelming extent and importance of the mythological content of one's religious belief.

W. Edward Deming stated in *Out of the Crisis* that the United States today might be the most underdeveloped country in the world.[7] The United States misuses and abuses the skills and knowledge of an army of employed people in all ranks of industry. The United States has used myths to manipulate her image around the world so that there is a misleading view of her strengths and weaknesses. Clearly, the United States is no longer the economic powerhouse it once was. The nation's prevalent metaphors are no longer functional or productive. The economic force has now shifted to Asia. Michael Hammer and James Champy, the consultants behind the reengineering craze, emphasized that managers must find new metaphors, because the old metaphors are invalid and counterproductive in the new global arena.

The productivity problems of America stem from symbolism and manipulation of the resulting mythology. The business community must understand this fact in order for productivity to become a reality. All metaphors used in the past must be discarded. New metaphors must be carefully examined and eventually eliminated. The business world, like other areas of human activity, has failed to see the need to eradicate myth, metaphors, and rituals. Instead, the necessity of these entities has

---

[7] Deming, W. Edwards, *Out of the Crisis*, Massachusetts Institute of Technology, Center for Advanced Engineering Study, Cambridge (1982).

been emphasized. As long as the business world sees the need for these symbol systems, the problem of productivity will continue to plague all aspects of American business transactions.

The use of consultants by the world business community has enhanced the manipulation and spread of myths and metaphors. As noted, Robert Reich, the former U.S. Labor Secretary, has called consultants "symbolic analysts". Symbolic analysts are consultants who make their living from manipulation of abstract concepts. This is the main reason why consultants and consulting firms have such a vast influence on who dominates the world. They take ideas and concepts and manipulate these myths worldwide. Consultants are used to introduce and reinforce ideas that the West needs to stay in power. This practice entrenches the West's power worldwide.

When W. E. Deming first revealed his Fourteen Principles, the United States was afraid to implement the principles for fear of upsetting its power structure and the U.S. obsession with racism and sexism. In Deming's philosophy, there were no losers, everyone was a winner. This concept is unheard of in the corporate Western world where having losers [those of non-white status] was business as usual. Although Deming never specified race and sex, it was obvious that if everyone would be a winner, Blacks and women would be treated fairly and promoted at the same rate as their white male peers. America and the West were not ready for this type of philosophy, and they fought diligently to see that it did not happen. Deming's principles were totally ignored and he was forced to leave the United States and go to Japan. His concepts, which were well received, shifted Japan's economic position to growth and power.

When Deming returned to the United States, the atmosphere was one of welcome. By then, the United States, with the use of her consultants, had become sophisticated enough to manipulate symbols. They created new myths and metaphors to guide the decisions of not only top managers in business but also the American public. American businesses saw Deming's success in Japan and wanted him to duplicate his philosophies in America. Unfortunately, they were able to accept Deming's principles and philosophies only after mythologizing them. They could feel comfortable with mythologizing the educational programs to fit their own agenda. If that educational program was to educate the employees, blacks and other people of color, then that principle could be used effectively in their business structure. This was a means of justifying the promotion and hiring of people due to the myth of intelligence as perpetuated in the book, *The Bell Curve,* by Herrnstein and Murray.[8] The book states that blacks are intellectually inferior to whites due to I.Q. tests and therefore cannot be as efficient and productive as whites. That is a perfect paradigm to show how the principles of education and self-improvement can be mythologized to distort and dilute its original intentions.

The I.Q. test is nothing more than the ability to reason in terms of symbol systems, which, in turn, means the manipulation of myths and metaphors. It is critical to remember that myths and metaphors are synonymous. This shows how the rest of Deming's Fourteen Principles were mythologized to fit the individual corporation. Deming was very disheartened at the attitude of not only American businesses but the business practices of the whole Western world. The practice of mythologizing ideas and concepts continues to hold sway in the top business schools in the United States. Ross Webber, chairman of the Management Department at the University of Pennsylvania, stated, "There has been a change in the myths that talented people in this new generation guide their lives by, and an entrepreneurial connection is a strong part of that mythology." [9] As long as corporate America and its leaders continue to place their hope for the future on new metaphors, the business community in not only the United States but also worldwide will never solve its problems.

The world economic community is suffering from a mythological approach to doing business. Because symbols are

---

[8] Herrnstein, Richard J. and Murray, Charles, *The Bell Curve: Intelligence and Class Structure in American Life*, The Free Press, New York, 1995.

[9] *Fortune*, "Kissing Off Corporate America," 2/20/95.

still the main ingredient and vehicle for making decisions, the best that top management can come up with are new metaphors as a basis for decision-making.

Tom Peters, in his best-selling book *In Search of Excellence,* says that American business schools must undergo sweeping changes to be relevant in today's international community. He talks about the emphasis of quantitative analysis in today's business schools without benefit of the so-called soft areas that a liberal arts education would provide.[10] But that barely touches the reality of the problems in our business schools. The business schools are looking for exactly what Peters talks about in a subsequent book, *Liberation Management,* when he echoes the phrase, "We need new metaphors." [11] Business schools have fast become what today's theological seminaries are -- factories that teach decision-making built on myth. Business schools worldwide produce new mythmakers. Until we change how we educate, the pedagogical problem that we face in the world today will remain unsolved.

In the book *In Search of Excellence*, Peters makes a strong case for the excellence of the companies he analyzed. However, he reversed his opinion years later when he realized the companies aren't so excellent after all. That would seem to follow the ineffectiveness of the business schools that he talks about.

It is clear that no one knows what he or she is doing in terms of productivity and management. That is why it is so necessary for the *Symptomatic Thought Process* to be applied. As an international management consultant, I see countless companies hiring consultants to implement so-called re-engineering. As stated before, re-engineering is nothing more than the manipulation of metaphors. Despite its use by corporations and

---

[10] Peters, Thomas J. and Waterman, Robert H., Jr., *In Search of Excellence: Lessons From America's Best Run Companies,* Warner Books, New York (1982).

[11] Peters, Thomas J., *Liberation Management: Necessary Disorganization for the Nanosecond Nineties*, Alfred A. Knopf, New York (1992) p. 370.

city administrations, re-engineering does not increase productivity.

If I seem to bring up racism throughout this book and not confine it to one area, it is because racism is present in all day-to-day activities no matter what those activities are, and I am writing the book as such. White companies use re-engineering for the simple reason that it sounds good and a white male thought of it. If the initiator had been a Black male, the topic would be oscure at best. Unfortunately, the business world rejects out of hand African input in any area that is deemed for whites only. This act of ignoring Black scholarship ultimately only hurts people who classify themselves as white. They could benefit greatly from concepts that they refuse to give credence to because the perpetuator of those concepts is not white.

It is very obvious that the problem-solving methods taught in business schools and practiced and honed in national and international corporations and businesses are impotent, a total waste of time, racially oriented, and ineffective to the highest degree. People who classify themselves as white put a spin on their behavior and activity that is filled with mythology. Unfortunately, a large percentage of Blacks all over the world buy it. That adds to the problem of Africans gaining a foothold in the worldwide economic community.

Several studies have been done on the so-called glass ceiling that Blacks face in the corporate world. The studies explore the rationale behind the force that keeps non-whites out of the upper echelons of management and power. They are never conclusive or seriously followed up. This results in a lukewarm attitude on the part of all concerned, especially senior management. In the vast majority of cases, these Blacks can never be creative or taken seriously. Black original thought is well received when the proposal is not advantageous to other Blacks. It does not matter whether those ideas have a possibility of rendering profit to a corporation.

In the international arena, Europe and North America feel threatened by Asia and its growing economic presence. Malaysia's Prime Minister Mahathir has done a great job in confronting the West on its racism and arrogance. Malaysia has formed productive alliances with other Asian countries and has recently forged a productive relationship with China. As Dr. Mahathir told a Malaysia-China forum in Kuala Lumpur, "We prefer to see China as a friend and partner in the pursuit of peace and prosperity in the region."[12] The international community must now take seriously the so-called developing world as it realizes its potential. Both Asia and Africa will indeed be a power to be reckoned with if they work together and form economic blocs. Meanwhile, Europe and North America have an agenda of destabilization when they view their economic position in jeopardy. It was fine for the West to form economic blocs that excluded people of color, but the moment people in Asia and Africa form blocs, the paranoia of the Western world raises its head.

When reading the literature on the economic situation in international business, white superiority always shows through. In structuring deals and making business decisions, the West must always view itself as coming out ahead. They have severe problems forming partnerships and joint ventures that will be fair for all. The white world must always be in front and their mythology does not allow them to share power equally. That came across abundantly clear in their agitation with President Mugabe of Zimbabwe regarding Zimbabwe's joint venture relationship with Malaysia. The West masked their irritation with technicalities, but it is clearly evident that their unhappiness comes from Asia doing deals with Africa, specifically Malaysia and Zimbabwe. There must be a serious and thoroughgoing Asian/African business connection if both regions are to realize their full economic strength. China and Malaysia have found a promising market in Africa. Africa is the richest continent in the world in natural resources and the Asian countries are taking advantage of the wealth in a way that will be advantageous for both regions.

---

[12] Cooke, Kieran, How Malaysia Discarded its Fear of China, *The Financial Times*, 2/10/95.

What must happen during the relationship between Africa and Asia is that proper and productive management must be in place to ensure smooth transactions and productivity of on-ground projects. It is imperative that decisions are not based on symbol systems that allow mythologically based transactions to undermine productivity. Nothing would make the West happier than failed business dealings between Africans and Asians. People who classify themselves as white have always thrived on creating situations of conflict between the non-white populace.

Doing international business based on mythological decisions is the way of doing business in the world today. However, I maintain that the future of doing business this way is extremely bleak. There may be some short-term gains and successes, but in the long term, I believe it to be destructive.

There has been book after book written by experts on international business from the business schools on today's economic climate. Lester Thurow, in his book *Head to Head*, talks about the economic battle among Japan, Europe and America. He criticized former British Prime Minister Margaret Thatcher for losing her job because of her inability to deal with the new economic realities, such as the integration of the European Economic Community. He faulted her inability to shift with the changing international community. Thurow failed to see that even the people who metamorphose under his scenario are not nearly progressive enough, for all that changes is the metaphor.

Head to Head is already obsolete. The coming economic battle is between Africa and Asia against Europe and the West. The economic battle is between people who classify themselves as white and the people of color throughout the world, with Africa at the forefront. If one is surprised that I mention Africa at the forefront, it is because they do not realize that this whole economic battle is built on the mythological concept of race, and whites see Africans as being the most threatening because we are the origin of all humanity. They possess the ability to produce color. That may be an unpopular assumption, especially to people who classify themselves as white, but the game is one of power and who possesses this power to determine the economic state of the world. This is something that people who classify themselves as white will not give up easily. There are other factors involved, of course, that have little to do with race. However, these other factors also originate in mythology. Therefore, they, too, can only be solved by the eradication of myth and the introduction of a symptomatic base of reference rather than a symbolic one.

The fact that we have been living in a world based on mythological assumptions has affected the productivity of the international business community. This is most unfortunate. I want it to be made very clear: the international business community cannot continue to do business as it has. The existing concepts for problem solving do not begin to address an escape from a mythological existence. All the studies by the so-called experts in management, quality control, and re-engineering are useless and impotent because of the continued insistence on manipulating metaphors, which reinforces symbolic behavior. This has not been addressed in any business conference or think tank. There seems to be a hard-core resistance to any change that would create an equitable system for everyone.

Asian and African countries must realize that their ultimate survival rests on their ability to discard their symbols, and by doing that, eliminating any decisions based on myth. That in itself will propel them to world leadership and power. If Europe and the West also follow that lead, we will experience a height of productivity as never before in the history of humankind. The choice is up to us.

One of the most intriguing and effective stories written was a book by Reginald Lewis, *Why Should White Guys Have All the Fun?* Lewis's autobiography tells the story of an African-American attorney who became a force to be reckoned with in the elite circle of Wall Street dealmakers. Lewis, who regularly topped a *Black Enterprise* list of Black entrepreneurs, understood the racism that he faced as he participated in the previously all-white-male world of arbitrage. Lewis not only bought McCall Pattern Company, but he successfully concluded a deal to buy Beatrice, the food conglomerate. His acquisition of

Beatrice catapulted him into the top of the world of international business. Lewis faced racism head-on and did not buckle. He forged solid relationships with other Blacks as he formed a team to confront all obstacles that were put in front of him to make him fail. His marriage to a Filipino attorney who understood the racism in America that they both faced further solidified his strength.

The Reginald Lewis story is a powerful narrative that is indeed symptomatic of the successes and failures of doing international business in a mythological world contaminated by racism. [13]

---

[13] Lewis, Reginald F. and Walker, Blair S., *Why Should White Guys Have All the Fun? How Reginald Lewis Created a Billion-Dollar Business Empire*, John Wiley & Sons, New York (1995)

CHAPTER FIVE

SYMBOLISM, MEDICINE, AND PSYCHOLOGY

A *Symptomatic Thought Process* completely rearranges the field of psychology. Both Carl Jung and Sigmund Freud have had a tremendous influence on psychology and psychiatry with their emphasis on symbolism and mythology. Jung broke ranks with Freud over the issue of symbolism and Freud's emphasis on dreams, symbolism and myth. Jung emphasized that the symbolic is essential for it illuminates the mythological content of human existence; and that we must live a mythological life to know who we are and to find out where we're going.

Jung's emphasis on the symbolic and mythological has done a profound disservice to the field of mental health. More than Freud, Jung emphasized the need for a symbolic and mythological existence. However, both Jung and Freud were incorrect. It is only because of their white skin that they have been received so positively. If Freud or Jung were Black, they would never have received the acclaim that they have received. I emphasize again: every area of life has its racial connotations. That racism, that system of symbols and mythology, is at the core of every decision that is made by people who classify themselves as white.

Black psychologists such as Amos Wilson have contributed to the field of psychology in a way that Freud and Jung never dreamed of. However, racist America makes sure that areas of research and study done by Blacks are not published by the major publishing houses, and in fact are ignored so that such information will be stymied and not reach the masses. We must remember that racism is a symbol system that has its origins in mythology, and in order to eradicate it, we must eradicate symbols and myth. We have to keep reminding ourselves of that fact because of the assumption in the dominant academic world that symbols and myth are permanent and can never be eradicated. If we fail to eradicate symbols and myths, we fail to eradicate racism. That must be stressed over and over again.

Derrick Bell, in his book *Faces at the Bottom of the Well*, talks repeatedly about the permanence of racism. He also states quite succinctly that Black people depend on a symbol system; he stresses that all we need to do is give Blacks symbols.[1] We believe that symbols are necessary along with the mythological system that they produce. If we fail to realize that symbols are the problem, racism and other results of that mythological system will eat us alive. Unfortunately, Black psychologists and psychiatrists still use the systems of symbols and mythology as vehicles for solving the mental health problems of Africans. Black scholars still operate under those mythological assumptions that originated in Africa.

Amos Wilson argues that European history is in some aspects true or false. This is irrelevant: That European history functions as mythology is the main point. Wilson did understand that mythology, period, is the guiding and ultimate point. Nowhere is that more relevant as we see European, or white, science functioning as myth. Because of its dependence on mythology and metaphor, science becomes impotent as it strives towards productivity. The function of mythology is to control and mold character and mythologize the world; in other words, to make symbolism a permanent part and focal point of the universe. Symbolism, when applied, evolves into ritual, which implants itself into the very fabric of civilization so that human behavior can be controlled. As a result, any creative, positive behavior that can civilize societies and eradicate injustice is stifled. With science and technology becoming more and more of a necessity, new metaphors are developed to insure the institutionalization of

---

[1] Bell, Derrick, ibid., pp. 23-24.

technology so that it can be utilized as a controlling influence in the world. The scientific effectiveness of metaphors is the goal of new concepts in management. These concepts are the major tools of consultants as they strain to utilize these symbol systems for their clients.

Symbolic behavior prevents us from gaining the full benefit of our current technological advances. Our use of the technologies becomes non-productive and ends up becoming high-tech mythology. Symbolic behavior renders technology, no matter how sophisticated, impotent. The bottom line is that if mythmaking Homo sapiens created and utilized technology, no matter how sophisticated, that technology becomes a technology of myth. In other words, technology derived from myth only creates new mythologies.

The purpose of metaphors in science is to manipulate the science so that it can be used in whatever way the user deems appropriate for his interests. That is one of the reasons why myth is so essential in a civilization that is unjust and barbaric: myth is necessary to misrepresent, corrupt, and misuse the truth. Therefore, whatever new technologies develop, no matter what they are, if symbol systems are in place, then that technology is suspect.

In the medical field, symptoms are a normal phenomenon. They are signs showing a state of health of people, be it mental or physical. In the physical disease state, the term symbol is never used as an entree to the discussion of disease or health. However, the term symptom is used repeatedly as not only an entree vehicle to the actual disease state but possible cure of the disease itself. The same process applies to the mental state as well. Unfortunately, productivity specialists have added the prospect of symbols to the mental health of humans the world over, and this has caused the vast array of problems we see in today's world.

With the work of Jung and others, symbols have been declared a natural and normal process of human thought. This view has retarded any progress of not only curative but also preventive measures of a healthy mental and physical environment. New findings in gene research have narrowed the gap between the physical and mental. After all, the brain is a part of the physical body.

Medical research has proven that mythological symbolism, which created racism, plays a large part in the trend of hypertension among African-Americans in the United States. Study after study has suggested that because of the stress that African-Americans experience in America due to racism, and because of inadequate health care and treatment plans due to racism, Blacks in America die sooner, and are likely to get cancer and heart disease at more than twice the rate of whites. If medical science were free of racism and its research institutions opened to the brightest minds that are unable to participate due to racism, there is no doubt some of our most serious and incurable diseases would be alleviated. We now see the worldwide effect of AIDS and the devastation it is causing. In Africa, the epidemic of AIDS is worse than anywhere else. Nowhere is it harder to get life saving drugs from the pharmaceutical companies because of overpricing and scarcity. All responsible health care professionals agree that racism, which produces poverty and ignorance, causes the catastrophic health problems among the non-white people of the world.

Some scientific physicians like L Luca Cavalli-Sforza are using their multidisciplinary background and scientific expertise to focus on genetics as a symptom to give us a more accurate account of history and race and the role it played in the phenomenon of human migrations. With the publication of *The History and Geography of Human Genes*, Cavalli-Sforza and his team have used the insights of disciplines such as archaeology, physical anthropology and linguistics to create a full-scale account of human evolution as it occurred across all continents. Cavalli-Sforza's findings are compatible with the findings of Cheikh Anta Diop in his book *Civilization or Barbarism*. Cavalli-Sforza's use of genetic data is compatible with the fossil record and the findings of African scholars the world over on the origins of the human race and their migrations. Cavalli-Sforza's use of DNA in creating an account of early human history is symptomatic as he uses genetic materials that are natural signs. Cavalli-Sforza's statement on race is very interesting. He states:

> The word "race" is coupled in many parts of the world and strata of society with considerable prejudice, misunderstanding, and social problems. Xenophobia, political convenience, and a variety of motives totally unconnected with science are the basis of racism, the belief that some races are biologically superior to the others and that they have therefore an inherent right to dominate. Racism has existed from time immemorial but only in the nineteenth century were there attempts to justify it on the basis of scientific arguments. Among these, social Darwinism, mostly the brainchild of Herbert Spencer (1820-1903), was an unsuccessful attempt to justify unchecked social competition, class stratification, and even Anglo-Saxon imperialism. Not surprisingly, racism is often coupled with caste prejudice and has been invoked as motivation for condoning slavery, or even genocide. There is no scientific basis to the belief of genetically determined superiority of one population over another. None of the genes that we consider has any accepted connection with behavioral traits, the genetic determination of which is extremely difficult to study and presently based on soft evidence. The claims of a genetic basis for a general superiority of one population over another are not supported by any of our findings. Superiority is a political and socioeconomic concept tied to events of recent political, military, and economic history and to cultural traditions of countries or groups. This superiority is rapidly transient, as history shows, whereas the average genotype does not change rapidly.

But racial prejudice has an old tradition of its own and is not easy to eradicate.[2]

As another important point, Sforza states:

> On the question of place of origin, the archaeological field is divided. A number of paleoanthropologists believe that modern humans originated in Africa, from which they spread to the rest of the world, beginning about 100 kya. This is in agreement with the genetic data. A fairly large number of anthropologists reserve their opinion. Another group believes that the evolution of *Homo sapiens,* and perhaps even its predecessor *H. erectus,* proceeded in parallel all over the Old World, and there was no expansion from Africa. The mitochondrial data are, at this point, the most useful in helping to reject this hypothesis given that the origin of extant types of Asian mtDNA is more recent than this hypothesis would imply.[3]

Cavalli-Sforza and his team have corroborated what African scholars have been saying for years. Of course, with the publication of *Civilization or Barbarism,* Diop had the last word on the African contribution to world civilization. The important factor to note is the use of symptomatic means in discovering the true history of the world. By using natural signs, we can bring a non-mythical, which means non-racist, approach to solving not only the problems of the past but the problems of the present and future.

---

[2] Cavalli-Sforza, L. Luca, Menozzi, Paolo, and Piazza, Alberto, *The History and Geography of Human Genes*, Princeton University Press, Princeton, N.J., 1994, pp. 19-20.

[3] Ibid., p. 155.

CHAPTER SIX

THE SYMPTOMATIC THOUGHT
PROCESS AND MYTH IN HISTORY

As stated before, Kast emphasizes the movement between symbols and symptoms. Her primary goal is to turn this symptom into a symbol.[1] This dynamic is rarely discussed in academic circles, but it is the key to the problems of humanity. It is extremely important to understand the interplay of symbols and symptoms. We understood that symbols are a necessary part of human development and brain activity. It is also stated that the whole of human history and the whole of life are symbolic.

To reiterate, a symptom is always a part of the original entity from which it has its origins. A symptom is never a substitute; it is a natural sign. The discoveries taking place use symptoms as the determining factor.

A team of scientists from George Washington University discovered tools made of animal bones that were used to catch fish some 90,000 years ago. These tools were signs that enable us to determine how early man formed sophisticated weapons to catch fish. These finds show that humans in Africa had invented sophisticated technology long before their European counterparts who had been credited with initiating modern culture. These tools are symptoms of the events that occurred so long ago.

To turn these symptoms into symbols would be to mythologize the dynamics of early man. This tendency to

---

[1] Kast, Verena, *The Dynamics of Symbols*, ibid., p. 137.

mythologize history is to create a history that can be manipulated to suit racist concepts and give misinformation about history itself.

Researchers Find Evidence of Early African Tools

Discovery Indicates Technology Developed There 75,000 Years Ahead of Europe, Asia

Reprinted by permission of Associated Press.

This also explains the work of Bruce Williams of the University of Chicago's Oriental Institute. Williams' analysis of a stone incense burner from a 5,100-year-old Nubian cemetery was rejected by some of his fellow scientists because of the implication it has for Egypt. The implication is that Nubian civilization not only preceded but gave birth to Egyptian civilization. The method which Williams used to analyze the incense burner from Nubia is purely symptomatic in that he used the results of natural signs to determine the age and importance of the incense burner and other findings that were discovered in Nubia. This led to a flurry of rejections and comments from Egyptologists, archaeologists, and other scientists who have always denied the Blackness of ancient Egypt and its Nubian origins. These scientists and their treatment of Egypt are an example of how one turns natural signs or symptoms into symbols. This is mythologizing history. In this case, because of the implication that Nubia was the creator of Egyptian civilization and the racial ramifications, scholars turned symptoms into symbols.

Reprinted courtesy of the Oriental Institute of the University of Chicago.[2]

Nowhere is that more clearly demonstrated than in the book *Black Athena Revisited,* edited by Mary Lefkowitz and Guy Rogers. In *Black Athena Revisited,* historical facts are mythologized to fit the racist thought patterns of their contributors. The most glaring example is the effort to turn the ancient Egyptians into a nonracial group of people, neither white nor black and with neither history nor ethnicity. In order to make these people nonracial, the authors had to mythologize their entire being. A reading of Diop suggests that there is no difficulty in identifying a German as a German or a Frenchman as a Frenchman, but when it comes to Africans and particularly the Egyptians, there is a great mystery in learning of their origins and race. With the work of Cavalli-Sforza, in *History and*

---

[2] Incense burner from Tomb L24 showing a royal sacrificial procession of three ships going toward a palace façade. Reprinted courtesy of the Oriental Institute of the University of Chicago.

Geography of Human Genes, it has been proven by DNA analysis that the ancient Egyptians were a Black population who had their origins in Nubia. Not only were the Egyptians a Black African people, but the whole of the human race has its origins in Africa and change was only superficial in terms of skin color as they migrated out of Africa to Asia and Europe.

The dynamics of DNA in determining the migration of human populations are the same as the dynamics of the stone tools that were discovered by the scientists from George Washington University. These dynamics are the analysis of natural symptoms or signs to determine the correct reading of history. When these findings are mythologized they are turned into symbols. It is yet another illustration of Verena Kast's statement that we insist on turning symptoms into symbols. As we go into the 21st Century we cannot afford to mythologize history for it will continue to destroy civilization.

Martin Bernal's book *Black Athena* is a perfect example of how a white scholar with access to African scholarship and literature uses that information to forge a somewhat progressive view of classical civilization. Bernal's ideas were debated, published, and talked about by the academic community, while the African scholars he quoted and learned from were ignored. This is the extent of racism and paranoia that white academia has shown toward scholars of color.

The debate on the origin and race of the Egyptians took an interesting turn when Egyptian immigrant Dr. Mustafa Hefny filed a lawsuit against the United States government for declaring him legally white. Caramel-hued, woolly-haired Hefny filed his lawsuit after a citizenship interviewer told him that he would become legally white after becoming a United States naturalized citizen. To decide his race, the interviewer used guidelines established by the Federal government's Office of Management and Budget, which stated that persons having origins in the peoples of Europe, North Africa, and the Middle East are considered white. In his suit, Hefny requested that he and other Nubians, who are in fact Egyptians, be legally declared Black. Hefny has darker skin than Colin Powell, his hair is kinkier, and he was born in Africa. Yet, in the United States he is declared white and Colin Powell is declared Black. Hefny maintains that the present United States system is a racist system. By denying the Black African origins of the Egyptians, Hefny states that for the last 400 years many white scholars have tried to resolve the logical dilemma of the ideology of white superiority and Black inferiority by separating Egypt from Africa and by claiming that ancient Egyptians were not indigenous Africans but a branch of the white race.[3] The new categories on race that have been added to the census forms only make matters worse; these categories are akin to the racial groupings used in South Africa. When whites are in a minority, they mythologize the facts of race to cause confusion among people of color. This is a perfect paradigm that shows the need for whites to turn symptoms into symbols so that history can be mythologized. This must cease in order for us to understand correctly the dynamics of civilization. One of the more overt and ludicrous examples of racism in Egyptology is exemplified in the catalogue, *Egypt in Africa,* published by the Indianapolis Museum of Art in cooperation with the Indiana University Press. In the introduction, Theodore Celenko stated that:

Although the early Egyptians were biologically African, the terms "white" and "black," particularly as viewed through an American social lens, are not appropriate labels to describe ancient Egyptian populations. It is probable that there was significant diversity among indigenous Egyptians, with variation, for example in skin color, nose width, and hair type. An enlightened view establishes that ancient Egyptians were not Europeans or Asians, and they certainly did not look like the Europeans or European-Americans who are presented as Egyptians in manifestations of popular culture.[4]

[3] Young, Wayne A. *The African Shopper*, June 1997.

[4] Celenko, Theodore, *Egypt in Africa*, published by the Indianapolis Museum of Art in cooperation with the Indiana University Press, (1996) p. 18.

Celenko goes on to state, "Ancient Egyptians, most notably during early periods, were biological Africans, that is, their ancestors originated within Africa."[5] Despite this, Celenko states that the early Egyptians could not be called Black. That statement shows you the length that Whites will go to denounce the Black involvement in building the first civilization. This kind of rationalization is the height of mythologizing scientific facts. Indeed, it shows the depth of this sickness in white academia as they continue to distort and degrade Africa's involvement in early history. It defies all logic and shows the desperate maneuvering of a people who classify themselves as White as they realize their minority status in the world. Their chief agenda is the continual degradation of African peoples the world over. It is very clear that the mythologizing of scientific facts reveals itself in the equation, turning symptoms into symbols, resulting in mythology.

We emphasize, yet again, that the racism inherent in the universe is due to mythology. We know that racism has its origin in mythology and symbolic thinking produces mythology. It must be emphasized that racism will continue to flourish as long as the human brain thinks symbolically and produces Homo sapiens as mythmakers.

Martin Bernal, in his book *Black Athena,* depends on mythology to prove the influence of Egypt on Greek civilization. Despite this, he also uses natural signs that reveal symptomatic connections between Egypt and Greece. For example, he states, "However, it is not merely the symbolism of the plaques that shows the intimacy of contacts between Egypt and Greece at this time. An analysis of the lead in the glaze shows that it came from Laurio." [6]

Bernal depends on the cultic, mythological, and legendary evidence to prove his thesis of Egypt's influence on Greece. However, the method of relying on mythology, no matter what

---

[5] Ibid., p. 18.

[6] Bernal, Martin, *Black Athena,* ibid., p. 54.

point one tries to prove, is faulty at best. That point was made very clear when Edith Hall stated,

> "Ethnicity could be proved or challenged by inventing genealogies and mythical precedents...In myth the ethnicity of heroic figures is remarkably mutable. Heroes can change their ethnicity altogether according to the ideological requirements of the imagination interpreting their stories." [7]

Like other scholars who are interested in the problems of civilization, Bernal gets caught in the dragnet that mythology casts. Hall goes on to state in her conclusion,

> Ultimately the decision whether to accept or reject Bernal's advocacy of the "ancient model" depends on whether we can accept his handling of ancient Greek myth. This would mean that we must accept that certain myths do contain unmitigated literal historical truths. *Black Athena* seems to present an unsophisticated view of myth in general, and Greek myth in particular.[8]

Actually, Bernal is not much help in his defense of Egypt and his insistence on Egypt's contribution to Greek civilization. He has not taken seriously the contributions of Cheikh Anta Diop and other African scholars. He is still hung up on the blackness of the ancient Egyptians and he fails to use scholars from Africa as his sources. Throughout Bernal's two volumes of *Black Athena,* he seems almost apologetic in his insistence on the contributions of Egypt. Remember: symbolism produces mythology, and mythology is used to distort scientific truth and fact.

People who classify themselves as White will have to get over their resistance to historical truth, especially when that truth

---

[7] Hall, Edith, *When is a Myth Not a Myth?* Bernal's "Ancient Model", Black Athena Revisited, Lefkowitz and Rogers, Ed. , p. 343.

[8] Ibid., p. 346.

has been documented clearly over and over again by science. The ancient Egyptians were a Black African people who look like any African American that walks the streets of the United States. Whites must get over the fact that Egypt's great role in world civilization was accomplished by black-skinned Africans who originated in the Nile Valley. These Africans were indeed the builders and founders of Egyptian civilization.

The major difference between Martin Bernal and Cheikh Anta Diop is that Diop depended on the symptomatic approach rather than the symbolic approach in his historical analysis. For Bernal to state in Volume One of **Black Athena** that Diop had only his faith in the fact that the Egyptians were Black is not only misleading but untrue. By his work on melanin and his analysis taken from the Egyptian mummies, Diop knew that the Egyptians were Black through scientific evidence. Diop did not have to mythologize his rationale to prove that Egyptians were of African origin. That, indeed, was a threat to white scholars who ignored and refused to quote the works of Diop. They ignored him because he was a Black African scientist who threatened their assumptions of not only African history but world history. As we see, all scholars must abandon the method of mythologizing. Mythology has no loyalties. As Mary Lefkowitz states, "Myth is a tricky object of historical inquiry."[9] It can be used by friend or foe and can easily devour both.

---

[9] Lefkowitz ,Mary, **Black Athena Revisited,** ibid., p. 15.

CHAPTER SEVEN

THE SYMBOLIC MYTHOLOGICAL ORIGINS OF RELIGION

All religion has its origin in symbols and myth, but the consequences of that reality have not been realized due to the universal treatment of symbolism and mythology. The works of Gerald Massey have shed a great deal of light on the problems of religion, symbol, and myth. As I stated in my book, *An African Answer*, because symbolism and myth created religion, religion has to be eradicated in the same way as racism. I am very sensitive to the shock waves that that statement will cause. But it must be clearly understood that the religions of the world, which indeed were created by the mythological systems of the world, have caused as much friction, death, and pain as racism.

Because of its implication for Africa and African people the world over, the work of Gerald Massey has not been taken seriously by modern white scholars. Like everything else, white academia has lost valuable information by the refusal to study the works of Massey. Massey emphasized the African origins of the religions of the world in general and particularly Christianity. Recent research and scholarship has proved that Africa was the home and creator of all world religions and those world religions originated from an African symbol system. Massey insisted that the Christian myth had its origins in the heiroglyphics of Egyptian mythology.

Charles Francois Dupuis was another scholar and revolutionary who, like Massey, insisted on the role symbol and myth played in all religions. Dupuis is not known today because his work challenged both Christianity and the myth of Greeks as a cultural beginning. His main work was *L'orgine de la Cultes (The Origin of All Religious Worship)*, in which he insisted that all symbols, mythologies, and religion could be traced back to one source and one source only, and that was Egypt. Like Massey, the work of Dupuis was largely ignored by scholars who were afraid of the truth and had no desire to see the truth recognized.

The theses of Massey and Dupuis have come out in bits and pieces in mainstream publications. Their work has found validity in some corners. In the prestigious newspaper, the *London Financial Times*, an article titled "Death Is Outwitted by Gods Reborn in Spring", lays bare the ideas of Massey and Dupuis. This article is so important that I quote it in its entirety:

> Universal symbols, far more ancient than Christianity, and their recurrence in the myths and folklore of the world is arresting and fascinating. Osiris of Egypt was imprisoned by his wicked brother, Seth, in a coffin. It was thrown into the Nile but was washed ashore and came to rest inside the trunk of a tamarisk tree. He was released from the tree, dying again and then being re-born, and a pillar of wood with four crossed branches -- the Djed column -- was raised upright as the sign of his life everlasting.
>
> Perhaps the drawing of parallels, in symbol and ritual, between Christianity and other mythologies might not have to be greeted, so many centuries later, with cries of outrage and apostasy from the literalists. Christian theology is, understandably, committed to the premise that earlier rituals were only anticipations of the coming of Christ, who was their apotheosis. Inevitably, it interprets other traditions in this light.
>
> When Mary, the mother, and Mary Magdalene are shown sorrowing on either side of the cross, they can be compared with the sisters mourning Osiris. And, as the Djed column was raised in ancient Egypt, after the Nile's

life-giving inundation, the people cried 'Osiris is risen,' just as, tomorrow, we proclaim: 'Christ is risen.'

Why, though, should either festival be *lessened* by comparison with the other? And, more than this, might not our own celebration -- with our advantage of the knowledge of both -- be enlarged by an awareness of the other? Not least on the ground that one way of loving our neighbors is to include their humanity within our own?[1]

Even though Massey and Dupuis are not quoted in this article, the article states what both men have argued over and over again: the Egyptian origin of Christianity.

The *Financial Times* also printed an article called "Religion: Are We Better Off Without It?" about the age-old dispute between science and religion. The conclusion is that science has the higher moral ground. As I stated in *An African Answer*, religion has caused untold conflict and harm in the world because of its symbolic, mythological origin. Whether in Africa, India, Bosnia, or Ireland, hundreds of thousands of people have been slaughtered and murdered over religious mythology. As the *Financial Times* article stated,

> [These people who do such acts] find their support from their myths and texts, among their priests and their silent co-religionists, because retribution is part of religion. In some devious way they are convinced that they are carrying out their god's will.
>
> Therein lies the moral advantage of science. Its morality is incompatible with such imperatives; scientific principles and logic cannot be construed as incitement to mass killings, or even individual murder. Science has had it backsliders: a few scientists have shown themselves capable of murder in the name of research, as happened in Nazi Germany and Japanese prison camps during the

---

[1] Cashford, Jules and Jones, J.D.F., Death is Outwitted by Gods Reborn in Spring, *Weekend Financial Times*, 4/3/94, p. X.

second world war...but today religion, with its backbone of retribution, jihad, crusade and battle, presents a threat to mankind that is quite as serious as any of the environmental and social perils attributed to science, and much more immediate.

A couple of years ago, I remember a scholar of Byzantine history saying he hoped that 'mankind will soon learn that religion is too important a matter to kill each other about.' It took me two days to realize how tragically mistaken that thought was. I wished him to say: 'if only mankind would learn that religion is too *unimportant* a matter to kill each other about."[2]

It is becoming increasingly clear that the symbolism that created mythological racism and religion has to be eradicated. All entities that have their origin in that symbolic mythology state will produce an environment of total destruction and barbarism. The Muslim Hindu riots that rage in India where hundreds were killed, and mosques and temples were destroyed, are due to that mythological symbolic religious force that compels people to murder each other in the name of their God.

There is not enough space to deal with all the theological ramifications of each religion. Religion is a very compelling force in our civilization and great emotions surround the aura of this mythological force. Indeed, mythology created all the world religions. As a result, religion has been a very confusing force in civilization. It would take volumes to go into a specific theology of the different denominations within the Christian church, as well as all of the theological technicalities of religion such as Judaism, Islam, Buddhism and all of the other religions of the world. But it becomes easier once we understand as a historical fact that all religions originated in Africa. Indeed, all religions came out of a symbolic mythological system. With this understanding, it is easier to analyze the symbol system that is called religion. As I stated in

---

2 Postgate, John, *Religion; Are We Better Off Without It?*, Weekend Financial Times, June 18-19, 1994, p. II-1.

my book, *An African Answer*, retired Professor Leonard Barrett of Temple University had the best definition of religion: "Religion is only a symbol system by which man searches for ultimate reality.[3] Symbol systems can never be a vehicle for man's experience with ultimate reality. All religions, as we know them today, must be eradicated along with racism. Religion that has its origins in mythology breeds a superstitious and symbolic behavior that motivates populations to kill one another in the name of their God.

---

[3] Ridley, Edgar J., *An African Answer*, ibid., p. 43.

Muslim protestors watching the Hindu temple Moti Lal in Lahore, 12/7/92, crumble to the ground as a result of its storming by Moslems, in retaliation for the destruction on 12/6 of Babri Mosque in India. Reprinted by permission of Agence French Presse.

CHAPTER EIGHT

SYMBOLISM IN ART

Art is one expression that shows a large amount of symbolic activity. Remembering that African people are the most symbolic people on earth, our art is the most symbolic. Nelson Mandela, in the foreword of the book *An African Dream*, stated that "John Muafangejo's prints are dazzling. He has gone beyond literal interpretation of ideas and takes the viewer in the realm of symbolism and dream." [1] The art of Romare Bearden emphasizes the symbolic metaphors of African-American life. But it was Muafangejo's works that stood out for their overt symbolic effect. Muafangejo stated, "When I see you like that and I want to draw you, I will add the more -- things, -- to make it more story, more power story." [2] Muafangejo gives the same definition as Jung of symbolism. Muafangejo is adding more story, which means he is adding more myth and metaphor to his drawings. Because Africans use symbolism abundantly in every area of our life, it comes out in our expressions, be it our relationships or our creative arts.

In an article in the *Financial Times* called "Symbolism of the Still Life", William Packer stated:

---

[1] Foreword by Nelson Mandela, *The African Dream: Visions of Love and Sorrow: The Art of John Muafangejo,* by Levinson, Orde, Thames and Hudson (1992), p. 7.

[2] Muafangejo, John ibid., p. 15.

The still life, the object taken from the natural world, closely observed and presented as itself, has its origins far back in classical times. It has been present ever since, as both pictorial prop and a reminder of the real and physical world. Also, its symbolic uses have always been seized upon, to reinforce the particular point the painting might wish to make -- the Skull for inevitable fate, the rotten fruit to signify the corruption of the flesh, the hourglass to tell us that all things must pass.

Indeed the game of iconographical interpretation of such still life elements has always been one of the principal pastimes of the art historian.

One of the several works by Zurbaran, which takes up an entire wall, is of a bird taking just a grape from a plate. But the bird is described as a linnet when it is clearly a goldfinch and the goldfinch, we remember, is a symbol of Christ's passion.[3]

What Packer described is the universal symbolism in art, much like the mythologist Joseph Campbell described the symbolism in the art works of Picasso and other vanguard artists in Europe.

Implementing a *Symptomatic Thought Process* and seeing things symptomatically will revolutionize art and the appreciation of art as never before. Symbolism leaves no prisoners. Its destruction affects all areas and disciplines. The world of the arts is just one victim. The appreciation of art and different art forms would be radically different when one sees them as symptomatic rather than symbolic. The elitism of some art forms would be eradicated. Paintings with highly ritualistic and mythological content would be clearly understood by those masses of people who would otherwise be uninterested. It must be understood that the eradication of all symbolic intent never eliminates the object that is symbolized. Instead, the object is realized and appreciated for what it is in its real and qualitative final state. This procedure

---

[3] Packer, William, Symbolism of the Still Life, *The Financial Times*, date unknown.

breaks the vicious circle that symbolism produces. That is, symbolism creates mythology, which leads to ritual and superstition, which ultimately leads to a distorted viewpoint created by the mythmaker.

Color has been used in a symbolic way beginning with the first symbolmakers to the present. When talking about color symbolism, we are not talking about using the color of something and symbolizing that color for something else. In other words, the reddish-brown color of the ancient Egyptians was the color of early Black Africans. Color symbolism involves seeing white as purity and non-white colors as having connotations of evil, death, and anything non-pure. Color symbolism revolves around the connotations of the colors and not, as some historians and Egyptologists have stated, the real color of the entity it portrays, but having that color designated to an individual as symbolizing something else. In other words, the color of the Egyptians who were painted Black signifies their real color as Black. Symbolism enters when color is mythologized as evil, bad luck and other negative connotations. Every entity in existence can be symbolized, that is, mythologized. Symbolization and mythologizing is a phenomenon of the human brain, a neurological misadventure.

In the entertainment field, symbolism has affected performance to a large extent. The music that is being performed is a symptom of the state of being of the larger society. Money is the guiding light as to what type of music is played and the kinds of performances that are ushered in by superstars. There has been a great deal of controversy about the lyrics of the so-called urban music that is performed mainly by Black artists. Rap music has taken a beating by people who hear the vulgarity of its lyrics and feel offended by its general message. Rap music with its highly symbolic content often has a sexual and sometimes violent nature. The linguistics of rap music are simply an expression of existential frustration, a symptom of the overall condition that Black people and others find themselves in. How one listens to the music determines how one is affected by it and how one sees the music and its value. By listening to the music symbolically one will see the music as vulgar and useless and will become very judgmental about its overall value. However, when one views the music symptomatically, one understands immediately that the music is indicative of the decadence in culture in terms of racism. This society's human relations are fraught with symbolic and mythological content. Even when the music was tranquil and existentially accepted by the masses as dignified and sophisticated, it had no qualitative effect on people who viewed it in the usual symbolic manner. Like the rest of the arts, music can have a very liberating effect on the performer and the listener if it is viewed symptomatically. When that happens, the forces that emanate from the music will be experienced in their qualitative wholeness because there is no symbolizing or mythologizing. Therefore, the quality and meaning of the music comes forth with great power and can be a pedagogical and existentially liberating force. Because symbolism is a neurological function of the human brain, anything can be symbolized and mythologized. It is simply at the discretion of the individual mythmaker. The entertainment field uses the highest technology and has a great penchant for mythologizing music, stage and films. So-called entertainment is used to spread and deepen racism as well as all the dehumanizing elements that are part of a mythological civilization. On stage and in film, the white power structure continues to portray Blacks, especially males, in a negative and subservient way. It is fine for Blacks to be comedians who make fun of themselves and their people for the benefit of white laughter and amusement. It is a part of the mythologization of the entire arts and entertainment field and is just another area where symbolic mythology has a tremendous impact.

CHAPTER NINE

THE SYMPTOMATIC THOUGHT PROCESS

The *Symptomatic Thought Process* must replace the symbolic thought process. Thinking symptomatically is our only chance to solve the problems of the world. Thinking symbolically has been the norm throughout human history and it has wrought havoc and disaster.

A symptom is a natural sign.

A natural sign is a part of a greater event. It signifies the rest of that situation of which it is a notable feature. It is a symptom of a state of affairs.[1]

The sign, then, is a concrete form -- a symptom of an invisible and inner reality, and at the same time the means whereby the mind is reminded of that reality. When one thinks symptomatically, one sees things as they really are, with no connotations. One sees things in their ultimate state. For instance, when a white person sees a Black person, they automatically begin to mythologize that person, which usually means, "This person is Black; he is inferior"; or "he will rob me"; or "he will not be able to perform this job because he is Black." That is thinking symbolically. Thinking symptomatically will simply mean, "Here is a Black person whom I see is Black." There are no connotations or added story behind 'this person is a Black man or woman.'

---

[1] Langer, Susanne, ibid., pp. 94-95.

That is a simplified way of showing how one thinks symptomatically. Thinking symptomatically rules out any desire or tendency to mythologize facts or add connotations.

Thinking symptomatically radically rearranges our behavior. It eradicates all of the illnesses and problems that are a part of symbolic behavior. This is a revolutionary way of behaving and making decisions that has no precedent in human history. It affects every area of human activity and changes the structure of civilization as never before. The potential for all disciplines is unlimited since it is the dynamic that eliminates worldwide conflict once and for all, whether it is based on racism or religion.

In the literature, symptoms and symbols are sometimes used interchangeably but there is a marked difference between what a symptom does as opposed to what a symbol does. In James Weldon Johnson's book, *Black Manhattan*, he stated, "The fourth of the great New York riots involving the Negro was really symptomatic of a national condition."[2] The use of the word *symptomatic* shows the connection to the ultimate reality of that situation. The statement shows the reality of that condition, and in fact, the Black man was an original part of a real condition that was occurring at that particular time. Whereas, if the word "symbolic" had been used, then that would have implied a mythological event. The word "symbolic" would have implied that Black people were not really a part of the original condition that caused the riots but could be mythologized in and out of that situation. The symptomatic condition can never be mythologized to mean anything else.

Another example of the way 'symptomatic' is used is by the Nigerian writer Buchi Emecheta when she stated that "the way Europe treats Africans is symptomatic for the whole European attitude towards Africa."[3] The reality is there for all to see -- the point of the statement cannot be mythologized.

---

[2] Johnson, James Weldon, *Black Manhattan,* Da Capo Press, Inc., 1930, p. 127.

[3] Emecheta, Buchi, as quoted in West Blasted for Ugly Image of Africa, by Holtkamp, Rieks, *The Final Call*, date unknown.

Professor Chuck Stone of the University of North Carolina at Chapel Hill gives another example. In his former newspaper column in the *Philadelphia Daily News*, Stone compared the community response to the brutal murder of a five-year-old Black girl vs. the community's response to a five-part newspaper series attacking the late Rev. Leon Sullivan and the Opportunities Industrialization Center (OIC), a long-respected institution in the Black community. The murder of the Black girl elicited a turnout of 150 people to a rally. However, the newspaper exposé drew 1,500 people to a neighborhood church, where they attacked "biased reporting." In describing these two "expressions of a community's anguish," Stone stated,

> "One responds to a symbol, the other reacts to a symptom. Magnificent and productive, the Rev. Sullivan is a self-help symbol in a powerful, racially segregated society. Impoverished and powerless, Naja [the murdered five-year-old] is a symptom of black indifference to crime and its casual tolerance for filthy housing and miseducation in public schools. Historically, blacks always knee-jerk to attacks on their beloved symbols while never mobilizing with the same ferocity to treat the symptoms of their self-imposed oppression."[4]

Ironically, a former colleague of Chuck Stone's at the *Philadelphia Daily News*, Larry McMullen, stated in a column titled "Making the Blacks Forget", "There is a common perception about Black people. That you can give them symbols instead of reality."[5]

The above statements express eloquently what needs to be emphasized over and over again. Historically, Africans and their descendants, which means all people, relied on and emphasized

---

[4] Stone, Chuck, Naja, OIC & Black Responsibility, *Philadelphia Daily News*, 11/25/80, p. 2.

[5] McMullen, Larry, Making the Blacks Forget, *Philadelphia Daily News*, 3/23/81, p. 2.

symbols as their primary mode of seeing the world. They replaced reality with symbols. McMullen's statement is very powerful; the offspring of Blacks worldwide (all people) used symbols instead of reality, which produced the mythological systems that we have today called racism, religion, and all other mythologically based philosophies. That is why it is essential for humankind to think symptomatically rather than symbolically. There is absolutely no other way to proceed if we are to survive as a civilization.

The continual experience of the *Symptomatic Thought Process* authenticates one's existence and eradicates the neuroses and all other ailments that are a result of symbolic behavior. While the dynamic of symbolism is to turn the symptom into a symbol, the dynamic of the *Symptomatic Thought Process* is to eradicate symbols and think symptomatically -- to turn symbols into symptoms.

Thinking symptomatically is simply seeing everything as it is. It allows one to face and experience reality in its qualitativeness without the baggage of mythology. That in itself completely eradicates mental illness in all its phases or forms. The *Symptomatic Thought Process* obliterates the problems that Freud and Jung tried to analyze; it eradicates all problems in every area and discipline. This is what makes it so imposing. It rearranges the structure of civilization and allows us to make assumptions from an entirely new foundation. When we see a tree, we see a tree. We do not see the goddess Nut in the form of a tree which was prevalent in Egyptian mythology. Thinking symptomatically, one is not afraid to confront reality. Any tendency to avoid reality runs a serious risk of developing into some form of mental illness.

The drawings that accompanied the works of Jung and his followers show the vast array of symbolism created by their patients. By analyzing the symbolism in those drawings, tentative diagnoses were made. This method continues to be practiced by psychotherapists today. Unfortunately, it does not cure mental illness or solve problems. We live in a civilization where people aren't getting well. It is a vicious circle: the very mythology that they depend on for cures is the very mythology that keeps people sick. The only way out is to eradicate that symbolic, mythological phenomenon and replace it with a *Symptomatic Thought Process*.

As we go about our tasks day after day, and as we go into any given situation, such as a business meeting where decisions have to be made that will alter the course of the economic system, it is imperative that a *Symptomatic Thought Process* be in place. The information we gather to piece together history is done by a symptomatic frame of reference -- such as the stone tools that were found in Africa that proves sophisticated technology started in Africa when it was previously thought to have originated in Asia or Europe. It was thought to have originated in Europe because of the mythological reasoning of white supremacy that Africans could never be at the forefront of sophisticated technology. When history is left to be interpreted through symbols and myth, literally anything can be said about what occurred from prehistory to the present.

While there are numerous recognizable examples of symbolic behavior, symptomatic behavior as a term is not only unrecognizable but also practically unknown. The *Symptomatic Thought Process* produces symptomatic behavior. Once we understand that symbolism causes racism, then it becomes very clear that mythology via symbolism must be discarded. By discarding symbols and thinking symptomatically, racism is automatically eradicated. This is a profound event. Of all the books that have been written on racism and race relations, none have understood the necessity of ridding the world of myth to eliminate racism.

Dr. Yosef ben-Jochannan, in his book *Black Man of the Nile and His Family,* defines race as "the mythical, non-scientific, classification of mankind into allegedly 'distinct groups'."[6] As noted earlier, UNESCO's volume *The General History of Africa* states, "The issue of race is not so much a

---

[6] ben-Jochannan , Dr. Yosef A.A., *Black Man of the Nile and His Family,* Black Classic Press, 1989, p. 81.

biological phenomenon as a social myth." With the elimination of symbolism, a *Symptomatic Thought Process*© is ushered in, and by doing that, racism is eliminated. If one insists on perpetuating symbolism and mythology, one is insisting on perpetuating racism. It is essential for Africans worldwide to eradicate myths from their lives so that they will be able to handle the stress of living in a racist world.

A study done by Harvard's School of Pubic Health and Kaiser Foundation Research Institute has stated that discrimination causes hypertension in Blacks.

> High blood pressure is far more common in Blacks than in whites, and it is also far more common in people of lower socio-economic status. About 37% of Black men over the age of 20 have hypertension, compared to 25% of white men. But 31% of Black women have the potentially life-threatening disease compared to 18% of white women.[7]

Another study done by the University of North Carolina cited the stress of adapting to white society as the major cause of hypertension in Blacks.

> The major study expressing that theory is University of North Carolina psychologist and epidemiologist Sherman A. Jones, who uses the term 'John Henry-ism' to describe a typical Black reaction to adverse living conditions -- after the fictional Black strongman who died pitting his sledgehammer against a steam drill. Mr. Jones says John Henry-ism is a manifestation of the struggle to get into the mainstream and is characterized by a belief that one can triumph despite the odds. It 'is a metaphor

---

[7] Brown, David, Study: Discrimination May Cause Hypertension in Blacks, *The Washington Post*, by 10/24/96, p. A4.

for the experience of Blacks in America,' according to Dr. James.[8]

These incidents show the mythological origin of racism and its tragic effects. There are only two ways to live: symptomatically or symbolically. We cannot do both. A study by Eric D. Peterson, a Duke University cardiologist, states that African-American patients with heart disease are 40 per cent more likely to die within five years of diagnosis than their white counterparts.[9] In other words, because of racism, Blacks' lifespans are shorter than anyone else in the world. Africans must live symptomatically rather than symbolically so that they can initiate the kinds of support systems among each other to fight racism and its tragic effects on all our lives. Even though mythology causes racism, Blacks who behave symbolically instead of symptomatically aid in their own demise. Indeed, mythology causes a behavior system that is unnatural and injurious to one's health.

The *Symptomatic Thought Process* makes it possible for individuals to interact with each other in a way that is sincere and without phoniness. It opens up relationships as never before. In corporations worldwide, there have been instances of not only racism but sexual harassment suits, employee theft and personality clashes. All these tend to destroy harmonious working relationships. Mythologizing brings about these problems, which creates an unstable and threatening atmosphere. Corporations do not need to re-engineer. They need to de-mythologize their behavior so that a symptomatic behavioral system can take its place.

Symptomatic Thought Process is recognizing people for who and what they are without mythologizing and adding connotations that have as their goal the destruction of the individual. When a Black walks in for a job interview and he is

---

[8] Williams, Linda, Stress of Adapting to White Society Cited as Major Cause of Hypertension in Blacks, *The Wall Street Journal*, 5/28/86.

[9] Winslow, Ron, Blacks Face Higher Risk in Heart Disease, *The Wall Street Journal*, 3/28/96, p. B3.

seen as a Black who is intellectually inferior because the interviewer has read he *Bell Curve* and bought into that I.Q. myth, that is symbolic behavior. However, when one looks at that individual for who and what he is and recognizes his Africanness, eliminating the mythologizing, one is thinking symptomatically.

Here as an illustration is the story of a Black MIT graduate, Omar Green, and the relationship he has with his boss, the CEO of Xionics Document Technology, Inc. This is a perfect illustration of a *Symptomatic Thought Process* being used in place of a symbolic one. This symptomatic behavior ultimately raises the productivity of the company and makes it possible for new ideas to form and take shape. The players are Robert Gilkes and Omar Green.

> Robert Gilkes is 58 years old, white and a British subject; his resume includes three years as a young magistrate in an African colony, overseeing the region's police, taxes and schools. Now chairman of Xionics, he is so imposing and aloof that some employees call him 'sir'.
>
> Omar Green is 27 and black; he was raised in Florida and graduated from the Massachusetts Institute of Technology. An engineer at Xionics, he usually sports three earrings, hair curls slicked with gel, baggy pants and oversized T-shirts.[10]

Mr. Gilkes, who was hired as a change agent for Xionics, does not look at Omar Green symbolically, but symptomatically. The article goes on to say:

> For Mr. Gilkes, Mr. Green represents technical and entrepreneurial thinking critical to his company's future, a chance to shake up resistant middle managers that have bucked many of his efforts to change Xionics. 'He can

---

[10] Kaufman, Jonathan Odd Couple: How Omar Green, 27, Became the Point Man and Protégé for a CEO, by *The Wall Street Journal,* 7/22/97, p. A1.

tell me things I am not seeing as a 58-year-old white man,' Mr. Gilkes says. [11]

All things did not go smoothly as there was some discomfort:

> One day, he [Omar Green] startled a roomful of senior engineers by questioning the power capacity of a Xionics computer chip. 'Who the hell is this loudmouth, smart-aleck kid?' Mr. Morris, his fellow engineer, recalls thinking at the time. Then, Mr. Morris realized the question was valid -- and hadn't yet been addressed. Mr. Green was later put in charge of testing the new chip, overseeing eight engineers, most of them at least ten years older. [12]

What is key here is that Gilkes did not mythologize Mr. Green's existence as a Black man. Instead, by making Green a member of an important team, Gilkes saw Green's potential contribution to the company. The article goes on:

> Mr. Gilkes says he sees Mr. Green as crucial in his drive to turn around Xionics. In his 2½years as CEO, Mr. Gilkes has taken Xionics public, doubled the number of employees to more than 200 and boosted sales to an estimated $40 million this year from $9 million in 1994. But the stock price, which started at $12 and soared to $22, is now below $11. Everything rides on the new chip and on developing new products.
> Mr. Gilkes has assigned Mr. Green to an elite team to develop an easy-to-use box that would give users access to their televisions, stereos, VCRs and computers, enabling customers to send and receive everything from music to computer files. [13]

---

[11] Ibid., p. A1.

[12] Ibid., p. A6.

[13] Ibid., p. A6.

This is a clear-cut example of productivity derived from using a *Symptomatic Thought Process*. There was no mythologizing, no connotations, things were seen as they really are in their ultimate state. This is extremely important. Gilkes sees things as they really are -- he sees reality -- he does not add to it -- he does not mythologize the facts. I cannot emphasize how important this is. If this situation were approached from a symbolizing point of view, things would have turned out much differently.[14]

With the rising use of advanced technological concepts and techniques, mythology and metaphors have been utilized at a faster and more pronounced way. Business school deans and so-called management gurus are extolling not only re-engineering, but new concepts built on changing and creating new metaphors. E-mail makes it easier to expand the distance of mythology vis-a-vis symbols. New technology has truly become the new mythmaker of the modern world. The Internet has produced new metaphors and is a very sophisticated way of spreading mythological systems around the world at great speed. The book *Internet Dreams: Archetypes, Myths and Metaphors* is a study of ancient myths, modern networks, and technology's use of symbol systems to produce complex systems of myth. As Scott D. N. Cook states in his chapter, *Technological Revolutions and the Gutenberg Myth*:

> *Exciting New Technology, Same Old Myth* -- The printing revolution is often evoked as a model for understanding the social importance of new technologies. The structure of technological revolutions implicit in such analogies is typically the Gutenberg Myth: a single technology being the sole cause of rapid and far-reaching social change. Throughout the 1980s, for example, the personal computer was depicted in the popular and

---

[14] Author's note: Xionics Document Technology has been acquired by Oak Technology.

scholarly press as single-handedly revolutionizing the whole of society. By the early 1990s, the same was being said about the "data superhighway." Not surprisingly, such discussions of exciting new technologies reflect the same sorts of historical and conceptual distortions found in nearly all references to the printing revolution.[15]

New technologies are not a solution to the problems that face mankind; they have not eradicated man's need to mythologize.

The scientific breakthroughs that have occurred in the past have improved some areas of human life, but they have not made the qualitative breakthrough that is necessary for civilization to be truly humanized. The *Symptomatic Thought Process* will enable new breakthroughs in all areas of science, such as physics, chemistry, molecular biology, and medicine. This will improve the quality of life worldwide. We can never be satisfied with the scientific and material wealth of the world when we have situations like Bosnia, Ireland, and Rwanda where people are slaughtering each other over symbolic, mythological differences. When our best minds can only come up with changing metaphors as a solution, then we are in trouble. The present rationale for solving problems leads to a vicious circle. The only certainty is the repetition of greed, racism, religious conflict, and man killing man such as the fighting in Ireland, Eastern Europe, and Africa.

One of the great concerns that are introduced with the elimination of symbolism is what it does to the religions of the world. As stated before, religion and racism are huge problem areas that are produced by mythology. Since all of the world's religions have their origin in mythological symbols, the elimination of mythological symbols is the elimination of religion. There must be religious tolerance in the world for people who do not have the same beliefs. Because religion has such a grand impact on

---

[15] Cook, Scott D. N., "Technological Revolutions and the Gutenberg Myth", *Internet Dreams: Archetypes, Myths and Metaphors,* Stefik, Mark, ed., Massachusetts Institute of Technology, 1996, p. 78.

people, it will realistically take time for people to come to grips with their individual beliefs, and they will have to make the decisions themselves as to how they deal with the mythology that permeates all world religions.

I would be remiss if I did not talk candidly about the implications of mythology and religion and the fact that religion has caused the loss of life of so many people around the world. Religion has been a tool that has been used to sanction racism, murder, sabotage and countless mythological sacrifices in various forms. These mythological sacrifices take the form of rituals that have cost millions of lives, all in the name of religion. For those who think symptomatically, it is up to them to decide how they will deal with their individual theological concerns.

Andrew Hacker gives a candid and thorough treatment of the effects of racism on the Black population of the United States in his book, *Two Nations*. This book honestly analyzes the racism of whites and how they perpetuate it on the African-American population. Here is one telling statement:

> Yet the actual Africa of today is not really the model Black Americans have in mind. Of much greater significance is how the continent is construed as a symbol: what it says about the human spirit, what it connotes as a way of life. It is more the Africa of history, before the imperial powers arrived. It is also an Africa of the imagination, of music and dance and stories. This Africa speaks for an ancestral humanity, for an awareness of the self, the bonds of tribe and family and community. [16]

That statement eloquently explains the symbolism that is active in the way Blacks perceive Africa. That is one reason why the behavior of Afrocentrists is no different than those who claim no commitment towards Afrocentricity. The symbolization of one's relationship to Africa does not produce a behavior that is

---

[16] Hacker, Andrew, *Two Nations: Black and White, Separate, Hostile, Unequal,* Charles Scribner's Sons, 1992, p. 13.

productive for the African continent. Those who espouse Afrocentricity depend on the extravagancy of their African garb and how many ankhs they can wear around their neck, and they behave no differently than those who have no such commitment. The failure of Black Americans to deal with reality is the failure to understand the importance of symbolism and the impact it has on their lives. It is only as we as an African people eliminate symbolic behavior and mythology can we begin to work together harmoniously instead of being buried in the intertribal conflict that has plagued Africans worldwide and allowed people who classify themselves as white to feed off us.

In his assessment of white liberals, Hacker goes on to say:

> Liberals account for most of the white faces in the audience for serious African and African-American music, art and theater. A similar interest holds for books by Black authors. Of course, white people of all ages and political persuasions are drawn to Black entertainers whether on television and movie screens or in athletic arenas. However, for those on the left, the attraction runs deeper than art and entertainment. For them, Africa - and much of Black America - remains symbolic of a mode of life that the white and western world has effaced or destroyed. [17]

As long as symbolism is allowed to flourish as a means of communication and a standard for relationships, we will continue to be a phony people, both Black and white, who are unable to rise above the effects of a universal mythological existence. Even though it is people who classify themselves as white who are the perpetuators of racism, we can never wait for white people to rid themselves of their racism. African people must rid ourselves of our symbolic behavior and mythological symbols that we hold dear. We must initiate a *Symptomatic Thought Process* that will compel us to liberate ourselves, make our own decisions, and

---

[17] Ibid., p. 55.

make a qualitative change in the world. It is imperative for African people on the continent and in the diaspora to work together and support each other as we fight against racism and all the forces that dehumanize us and people all over the globe. This can only come about by eliminating our symbols and our penchant for making decisions based on myth. We can then initiate a *Symptomatic Thought Process* that will compel us to work harmoniously with each other, love and support each other as we struggle and fight for worldwide liberation in a world that is increasingly becoming barbaric.

It is very realistic and sane to envision a world that for all practical purposes has no racism. What kind of world would that be? Those who feel that racism will always be prominent feel that way because they refuse to relinquish their myths. They continue to hang on to their symbol systems. These are the people that will kill, discriminate, and destroy in the name of their God. It goes hand in hand.

If one sees mythology as a permanent part of culture then one sees racism as a permanent part of culture. The refusal to eliminate mythology is a refusal to eliminate racism.

CHAPTER TEN

SYMBOLISM REVISITED

In 1982, I wrote a paper titled *The Neurological Misadventure of Primordial Man*, where I stated that:

> African people were the first people to create symbols and symbolic behavior. They produced an abundance, and indeed, an overabundance, of rituals and superstition which led to their downfall. Subsequently, Arabs and later on, Europeans came in and destroyed these African people and their culture, and that destruction is continuing as we live today. [1]

I also stated in that paper that traditionally symbols have been thought to be a natural process of brain function and brain development. I concluded by stating:

> Non-symbolic African man will cease to be fooled by symbolic manipulation. He will be able to deal with his experiences with a reality that can only come from seeing things symptomatically rather than symbolically. [2]

That paper was a thesis that I presented to Dr. Cheikh Anta Diop at the Radiocarbon Laboratory in Senegal, West Africa. I then presented that same paper to the African Heritage Studies

---

[1] Ridley, Edgar J., *The Neurological Misadventure of Primordial Man*, The National Newport News and Commentator, Newport News, VA, p. 1.

[2] Ibid., p. 11.

Association conference in New Orleans on a panel chaired by the late dean of African Studies, Dr. John Henrik Clarke. Following my presentation, Dr. Clarke stated that he was not prepared to comment on the paper because he did not know enough about the subject matter. That shows you how unfamiliar the discussion on symbolism and brain activity is.

Terrence Deacon, a world-renowned researcher in neuroscience and evolutionary anthropology, wrote *The Symbolic Species: The Co-Evolution of Language and the Brain,* in which he addresses the dynamics of symbolism on the brain and language. Deacon's book is extremely technical but readable with a little effort. His main thesis says "Language reflected a new mode of thinking: symbolic thinking.[3] Of course, Deacon feels that symbolic thinking evolved naturally and must be continued if Homo sapiens sapiens is to live productively.

The first problem with Deacon's thesis is when he states that language is symbolic. Language is not symbolic; language is a symptomatic feature of Homo sapiens. This is especially true when we remember that symptoms are natural signs, and "a natural sign is a part of a greater event or of a complex condition, and to an expert observer, it signifies the rest of that condition, of which it is a notable feature. It is a symptom of a state of affairs."[4] In other words, language is an important part of Homo sapiens sapiens. It is a natural sign when used normally. Language only becomes symbolic when it is manipulated to become myth and metaphor. However, Deacon is on target when he asserts:

> One of the most difficult social symbolic relationships to mediate is peace. This is not so much because of a conceptual difficulty, but rather because of the high potential and high cost of deception. The problem of establishing peace after a period of war also

---

[3] Deacon, Terrence W., *The Symbolic Species: The Co-Evolution of Language and the Brain*, W.W.Norton & Co., New York, 1997, book jacket.

[4] Langer, Susanne, ibid., pp. 94-95.

demonstrates the importance of the indexical sub-structure of a symbolic social relationship. Agreements and contracts concerning future behaviors and obligations are intrinsically symbolic. Because the referential link between symbols and their objects is indirect, the very same features that make symbolic reference the only means for definitively representing something that is as abstract and virtual as a promise or contract also open the door to misrepresentation and falsehood. The problem lies in determining whether a symbolic gesture for peace is made in earnest, particularly when it comes from a former enemy who in other circumstances may have employed misrepresentation and misdirection as a ploy.

An interesting example of this comes from the Yanomamö Indians of the rain forests of Venezuela and northern Brazil. These slash-and-burn agriculturists live in small, lightly fortified villages with nearby gardens. Such villages are almost constantly at war with each other, and skirmishes are often initiated by surprise attacks. But there are times when it is necessary to cooperate with one's neighboring villages: for example, when a garden is becoming overgrown and unproductive, soon it will be necessary to abandon one village and create a new one. At times like these a Yanomamö group might be at high risk of attack. How do you make peace in order to gain allies at this crucial time and decrease the chances of attack? Peacemaking is a difficult problem no matter what the conditions. It is a situation where the major communicative problems are not due to a lack of symbolic activity, but rather because no one is sure that others are using the symbols honestly. The situation is similar to not having reliable symbolic reference at all. What is necessary in order to reestablish reference -- to ground it in the real world so to speak -- is a reconstruction of the symbolic relationship from its component indexical relationships. Demonstrating true symbolic reference is analogous to establishing symbolic reference in the first place. Symbols refer to relationships among indices, and are learned by first establishing these indexical associations. Regrounding questionable symbolic reference similarly requires a return to the indices on which it is based. So the question is: What system of indices does peace represent? Indications that members of the groups are not hostile. Indications that they would not engage in violent behavior even if the opportunity were to present itself. And possibly indications that they are disposed to cooperate with one another. Unlike symbols, indices are part of what they refer to, and this makes them reliable in ways that symbols are not.[5]

Because of our symbolic behavior and mythmaking, global conflict is rampant. Symbolic behavior and symbolic relationships are, at best, unreliable and phony. As Deacon stated, symbols are not reliable. As I stated in my paper, *The Neurological Misadventure of Primordial Man*:

I realize that the proposition that symbolism from a neurological starting point is a misadventure and must be abandoned presupposes a thought pattern unheard of in world academia. However, I maintain that the mind process that crystallizes certain aspects of energy from our experiences and creates symbols is a brain misadventure that disallows any possibility of creativity, because the experiences that the brain crystallizes cannot be relayed with any kind of reality. The correct neurological adventure that takes place is that the brain crystallizes, if anything, natural signs from our experiences. These natural signs, or symptoms, create reality, or bits of reality, from ultimate reality, or from those experiences that are an original part of that core

---

[5] Deacon, Terrence W., ibid., pp. 403-404.

reality. I want to emphasize that the alternative to symbols and thinking symbolically, is symptoms, or, thinking symptomatically.[6]

Deacon's work hopefully will help illuminate the importance of symbolism, even though his main thesis is strictly along the traditional line of thought in terms of the dynamics of symbolism. Deacon also states that Homo sapiens is truly Homo-symbolicus. But when Homo-symbolicus corrects his neurological misadventure, he becomes Homo-symptomaticus. Homo-symptomaticus is the true, non-symbolic Homo sapiens sapiens. He is African man, as we all are African. His phylogenetic history is compatible with the fossil record. This is the description of the complete, healthy human.

As I have stated in my book, *An African Answer*, and as was stated in Verena Kast's *Dynamics of Symbolism*, what happened in early history and is happening now is that people are turning symptoms into symbols. As we know, this is a neurological misadventure and is also the beginning of the life of rituals. Deacon also attempts to turn a symptom into a symbol when he states:

> Even a symptom can refer to something other than itself and other than the state of the body that produces it. Take, for example, human laughter: a symptom of being in a highly amused state of mind. Laughter is an excellent example of a human innate call (I will return to analyze both the evolution and physiology of this call in later chapters). Like other calls it need not be intentionally produced; it often erupts spontaneously even when we would rather suppress it, even though it can also be faked (with variable success) if the social context demands. For the most part we tend to think of it as a way to work off feelings inspired by a joke or an awkward social situation. But laughter also refers to

---

[6] Ridley, Edgar J., *The Neurological Misadventure of Primordial Man,* ibid., p. 9.

things as well. For example, when someone walks into a room laughing, it suggests that they probably heard or saw something funny just outside, before entering. The laughter points to this something else that caused it. And it specifies some of the characteristics that this cause probably exhibits; specifically, it was not a source of sorrow, not a disgusting or repulsive scene, not a real threat, and so on. It categorizes the event that induced it by virtue of what the laughter tells us about the state of the laughter. It points to a definite class of experiences that are deemed funny. But notice how different the reference to the same event is when the person stops laughing and says, 'I just heard a great joke.' Alarm calls refer to objects the way laughter does, not the way words do.[7]

Also, Deacon describes the process of changing metaphors that is so much a part of the reengineering effort used in the corporate world today. As I have stated before, reengineering is nothing but the manipulation of symbols, and we know symbols equal myth and metaphor.

The process of discovering the new symbolic association is a restructuring event, in which the previously learned associations are suddenly seen in a new light and must be reorganized with respect to one another. This reorganization requires mental effort to suppress one set of associative responses in favor of another derived from them. Discovering the superordinate symbolic relationship is not some added learning step, it is just noticing the system-level correspondences that are implicitly present between the token-token relationships and the object-object relationships that have been juxtaposed by indexical learning. What we might call a symbolic *insight* takes

---

[7] Deacon, Terrence W., ibid., p. 57.

place the moment we let go of one associative strategy and grab hold of another higher-order one to guide our memory searches.[8]

The human brain's natural inclination is to think symptomatically. It is a distortion of the natural processes that start symbolic thinking. It is only a matter of time when the people of the world realize that symptomatic thinking is not only necessary but a must if we are to survive in a universe that is both complex and brutal. Will the world reject concepts that create a universe of justice and peace? Or is the fear of sharing power with a majority non-white population too threatening and undesirable to fathom?

The overwhelming majority of scholars today see symbols as a way of life. Edward Whitmont states: "The whole of life can be seen as a symbolic quest." [9] Barbara C. Sproul states, "Myths are still valid because they show how life is a symbol to be lived." [10] Joseph Campbell states, "Civilizations are grounded on myth" [that is, symbol].[11] So it is well understood that life itself is considered a symbol. Deacon's response to this is as follows:

> Perhaps this is because the savantlike compulsion to see symbols in everything reaches its most irresistible expression when it comes to the symbolization of our own lives' end. We inevitably imagine ourselves as symbols, as the tokens of a deeper discourse of the world. But symbols are subject to being rendered meaningless by contraction, and this makes alternative models of the world direct threats to existence.[12]

---

[8] Ibid., p. 93.

[9] Whitmont, Edward C., ibid., p. 136.

[10] Sproul, Barbara C., *Primal Myths: Creation Myths Around the World*, HarperCollins, San Francisco, 1991, p. 30.

[11] Campbell, Joseph, *The Power of Myth*, p. 72.

[12] Deacon, Terrence W., ibid. p. 437.

This is the dilemma. While scholars are calling for a symbolic existence, Deacon eloquently addresses the obvious pitfalls for such a state of being. Deacon's book is valuable for its emphasis on the neurological dynamics of symbolism and how critical that area of study is if we are to begin to solve any of the problems we face today. We must get the masses of people to focus on the study of symbolism and its interplay with symptoms. Although it is clear from Deacon's remarks that the symbolic lifestyle leaves a lot to be desired and has caused severe problems in civilization, Deacon still sees symbols as a permanent and normal vehicle from which humans live a mythological existence.

There can be no other way to look at this. Symbols must be discarded. The rationale that goes into supporting a symbolic existence is as absurd as calling the Egyptians a white people. The rationale for saying that the Egyptians were neither white nor Black, and were not Asian or Semitic, is as ridiculous as proposing the symbolic life as a life to live in order for man to be productive and creative. That rationale results in a vicious intellectual circle based on ridiculous, that is, mythological assumptions that are a product of symbolic thinking. The intellectual rationalization within academia results from a pedagogical process that is firmly rooted in mythological symbols. If we are to advance as a civilization, this type of thinking must cease.

The City of Richmond, Virginia hired consulting firm KPMG for a reengineering project with the Commission for Reengineering City Government. The subsequent report stated that Richmond had the lowest employee morale of any city the consulting firm had studied. It found that "racial discrimination, in hiring and promotion, is the order of the day. The only requirement for leadership positions is to be white and male."[13] It also found, "Morale sucks. And management not only doesn't care -- they seem to do everything they can to exacerbate the

[13] Street Talk, "City Morale Seems Nothing to Cheer About", *STYLE Weekly*, Richmond, VA, p. 6, 8/5/97.

problem." [14] The response to the report, as expected, was to mythologize the findings: "In any organization as large as the City of Richmond, you're going to have somebody who's unhappy. But that does not mean that everyone's unhappy." [15] The consulting firm's contract was not renewed for the second phase of the study.

By mythologizing the report, the concrete issue of racism and incompetence was pushed under the rug. Reengineering can never be successful by rearranging metaphors. The metaphor of racism -- the myth of racism -- must be eliminated. That is why reengineering has not succeeded: its practitioners don't understand that the mythology in reengineering must be eliminated. We cannot get around the fact that people just do not want to deal with the myth of racism. Whites always want to avoid this core issue of racism because it is uncomfortable, and they are still in a state of denial. Thinking symbolically produces racism, incompetence, sexism and the manipulation and rearranging of myth; thinking symptomatically eliminates myth, racism, and all the elements that make up for a dehumanizing civilization.

I have been asked: what does it mean to live a symbolic existence rather than a symptomatic existence? Living a symbolic life is living a mythological existence based on racism, dehumanization, constant tribalism, religious conflict, entities that tear down the very fabric of civilization. We cannot live out our life symbolically and have a civilized society. We can never accept these elements as a permanent part of our society and expect to flourish as a just civilization.

African entrepreneur Noah Samara has created one of the most ambitious radio communication projects in history. Samara, chief executive of WorldSpace, realizes that lack of information equals ignorance. His company provides a direct-to-receiver satellite audio service to the so-called underdeveloped world: Africa, the Middle East, Asia, the Caribbean, and Latin America.

[14] Ibid., p. 6.

[15] Ibid., p. 6.

These areas lack up-to-date information that would help them increase their productivity. By using satellite technology, WorldSpace is remedying the problem of information blackout in those areas.

Noah Samara is acting symptomatically as he focuses on the real needs of the vast majority of the people on the earth. It is ambitious and revolutionary business concepts like this that make for productivity and efficiency on a worldwide basis. Like Reginald Lewis, Noah Samara refused to be manipulated by the myths that are intentionally created to stop productivity and progress for African people. It is especially important for Africans who have been victims of the very myths that they created to realize that these myths have been propagated and refined by the white population to destabilize the world and strengthen white racism. WorldSpace is one example of how thinking symptomatically uses technology, not to perpetuate myth, but to perpetuate true information and education that has the possibility of liberating the areas of the world that are enslaved to myth. WorldSpace shows that technology can be utilized in a way that does not include symbolic dependency.

The dynamics of the *Symptomatic Thought Process*® on the individual brain is the most dynamic and important experience one could ever have in his lifetime. The human brain processes energy and entities continually. That process is the key to the decision-making and behavior of the individual. The stimuli processed by the human brain become symptoms of a state of affairs. Those symptoms are always qualitatively ultimate in their character.

> "The correct neurological adventure that takes place is that the brain crystallizes natural signs from our experience. These natural signs, or symptoms, create reality, σ bits of reality, from ultimate reality, or from those experiences that are an original part of that core reality."[16]

---

[16] Ridley, Edgar J., *The Neurological Misadventure*, p.9.

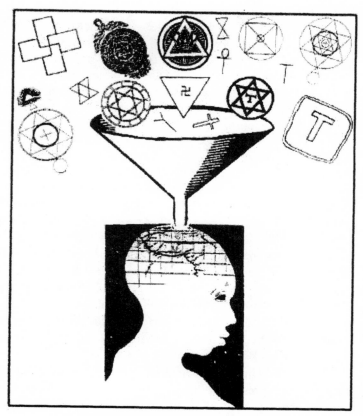

Diagram courtesy of E. Curtis Alexander, Ed.D.
Reprinted with Permission

The figure shown above depicts matter or stimuli being funneled into the human brain, which are natural signs. These natural signs are not symbols because they have not been processed yet neurologically. Only the human brain can create symbols. There is no such thing as symbols existing before they are processed within the human brain. All entities that exist before being processed within the human brain are natural signs.

What does that mean for us as we go about our daily lives? This means that whenever we see anything, we look at it without the mythological symbols that produce connotations. We do not think in connotations. We see things as they really are in their ultimate state as they are presented to us, and we do not mythologize about these entities. Once we mythologize, that creates the neurological misadventure. We have stated before and given examples of what that mythologizing turns into. The connotations disappear when we process these entities symptomatically. To think about living in a civilization where there is no racism; there are no religious wars; just those two phenomena will produce a peace and tranquility that the world has never known. It all starts with that process within the human brain that all individuals experience. That affects every area of human activity. This *Symptomatic Thought Process®* would mean that people would be free to do the kind of medical research to cure the world's diseases. Environmentally caused diseases would be eradicated. We would do business in a completely different way, where the level of productivity and business deals transacted would produce a quality of life that was thought to be unattainable. The possibility of such an existence is exciting to say the least and it can happen if the *Symptomatic Thought Process®* is implemented and practiced.

There are numerous examples that show how thinking symptomatically results in a positive outcome and unleashes decisions that are void of myth. A New York Times article describes Blacks in major corporations who find it much healthier and wiser to leave their hostile corporate environments to run their own businesses or work for other Black firms:

> Pamela Anderson sells delicately hand-painted wine glasses, oak counter stools, and other housewares. Though the work might seem a substantial comedown from her former job as an assistant vice president of First National Bank of Chicago, the 31-year-old Ms. Anderson is much happier, smoking less, and exercising more now

that she no longer works for a predominantly white organization.

James Hill, also black, routinely spurns executive recruiters who want to place him in a job he once lusted after: vice president at a big corporation. He prefers being President of Burrell Communications Group's public-relations unit. Mr. Hill, 40, jumped two years ago to Black-owned Burrell from Sara Lee Corporation, where he was public-relations director. One reason: he felt uncomfortable as the only Black manager at Sara Lee headquarters.

Ms. Anderson and Mr. Hill represent what many people believe is a widening exodus of talented Blacks from mainstream white businesses and professional firms. The primary reasons for leaving are racial: Some blacks say they are pushed by perceived blatant racism at the white companies or by more subtle complaints; others say they are pulled by a desire to help black businesses prosper.

'We just want to be treated like everyone else', says Phillip Turner, 34, who left the U.S. Attorney's office in Chicago to work at a Black law firm at a lower salary.[17]

This is a perfect example of Blacks breaking the myth that we have to work for white corporations to be successful. Rather than symbolically looking for white corporate America to be our saviour, we must take it upon ourselves to solve our own business problems and support each other economically. This is behaving symptomatically. In the same article,

"Edward M. Jones, Jr., a Black management consultant in South Orange, N.J., states, 'It's mandatory that Blacks have the choice to succeed in major

---

[17] James Frank E., More Blacks Quitting White-Run Firms, *The Wall Street Journal*, 6/7/88.

corporations. If we're locked out of major corporations, we're locked out of America.'[18]

Mr. Jones is a perfect example of someone thinking symbolically and mythologically. Unfortunately, he feels that we need to be sanctioned by the major white corporations or else we cannot succeed in America. Thinking symbolically produces the kind of mentality which is the same state of mind that has destroyed Africa.

Interestingly, Fortune magazine talks about white business school graduates leaving corporate America to form their own companies. Their reason for leaving is "there has been a change in the myths that talented people in this new generation guide their lives by. And an entrepreneurial connection is a strong part of that mythology."[19] This group of so-called talented people have restructured and changed their myths. This means that they're developing new companies on their own but they will still have the racism that the larger corporations have. They've just rearranged their myths and metaphors so that their rituals will be more compatible with their lifestyle.

Another example of how symptoms are used is in an article from a daily paper from Singapore. The article states:

'Nearly all children who are sent to the accident and emergency departments in British hospitals with head injuries have an X-ray taken, but only a tiny number show fractures, and X-rays are even less useful for predicting any damage to the brain caused by head injury,' British researchers reported in the Lancet.

The researchers said symptoms of brain damage, such as headache, vomiting, drowsiness, irritability and dizziness are a more sensitive way of predicting injury than an X-ray.[20]

---

[18] Ibid.

[19] Labich, Kenneth, Kissing Off Corporate America, by *Fortune,* 2/20/95 p. 44.

[20] Wee, Lee, "Changing World", *The (Singapore) Straits Times 4/2/97.*

The above demonstrates how symptoms are used in medicine as an analytical tool that supersedes some of the mechanical technology that we often take for granted as foolproof. This is why I repeat that thinking symptomatically is a natural neurological process. Symbols are not. They have never been, they are not now, and they never will be a valid and natural phenomenon that can be a catalyst for productivity and human advancement.

A New York Times article, "Dust and Sea Mud May Link Human Evolution to Climate," states,

> From the sea floors around Africa, scientists have found intriguing evidence about forces that may have shaped the evolution of humankind. Cores drilled out of the sea bottom contain layers of dust blown off the surface soils of Africa. Analyzing these layers of dust back to five million years ago, a critical period in hominid evolution, paleoclimatologists have constructed a picture of changes in climate and vegetation, matching them to major developments in the evolution of humanity's ancestors as shown by the fossil record.
>
> They find that a major cold, dry spell 2.8 million years ago forced woodlands in sub-Saharan Africa to yield to grasslands. Animal species, including prehumans, would have had to undergo major adaptations to accommodate to this shift in their environment. It is known that around this time, the ancient prehuman line apparently split into at least two branches. One was the genus Homo, which led in time to modern humans. The other was a kind of ape-human, known as Australopithecus robustus, whose line ultimately became extinct. A second dry, cool period occurring about a million years ago coincided roughly with the emergence of Homo erectus, the immediate ancestor of Homo

sapiens, as the sole representative of the hominid line and
its expansion out of Africa to the rest of the world.[21]

The dust in the sea mud is a symptom of a state of affairs, a
catalyst for the correct process of analyzing human evolution in
prehistory. It is void of any mythological interpretation and goes
straight to what we know about human evolution.

Another recent discovery of ancient footprints in Southern
Africa once again proved that by discovering and analyzing
natural signs, we are able by symptomatic evidence to tell the
story correctly of what occurred in early history. The footprints
of a Black African, in all probability a woman, were found in
Southern Africa by paleontologists at the University of
Witwatersrand in Johannesburg, South Africa. Lee Berger and
David Roberts said that these were the footprints of the earliest
modern people. These signs of early Africans are natural signs
that are symptomatic evidence that, once again, proves that
humanity comes from Africa.

The crucial element in the *Symptomatic Thought Process* is
behavior. There is a marked difference between behavior that
derives from a symbolic thought process and behavior derived
from a *Symptomatic Thought Process*. The behavior of people
acting symptomatically is one that is void of the elements that
have traditionally caused world conflict. How one behaves is a
critical predictor of whether we have a civilization or a barbaric
world. Symbols were never thought to be critical in man's
negative behavior because symbols were thought to be a natural
process. However, as we now know, symbols and a symbolic life
are the reason for man's negative behavior around the world.
Symptomatic-behaving man, that is, Homo-symptomaticus, is free
of racism, superstition and is able to make judgments that will be
effective in humanizing civilization.

As we assess one of the great paradoxes of Africa -- that its
people are for the most part desperately poor while its land is

---

[21] Stevens, William K., Dust and Sea Mud May Link Human Evolution to Climate,
The New York Times, p. C1, 12/14/93.

extraordinarily rich -- behavior patterns are crucial. It is the opposite in East Asia. The region is mostly poor in resources, but over the last few decades has enjoyed one of the greatest economic boons in history. Ineffective behavior determines whether a country or continent is productive or not. Countries who adopt the *Symptomatic Thought Process* will thrive no matter what their natural resources. This is why it is critical that Africa, which is the richest continent in the world, initiate symptomatic behavior so it can utilize its great natural resources efficiently and productively.

One of the most rewarding aspects of thinking symptomatically is existential tranquility. One may be unhappy with the world situation, but inwardly, one is at peace with themselves and their behavior. Thinking symptomatically authenticates one's existence.

Africans not only were the first people to inhabit the world, but they were also the first to build other countries and civilizations. As Ivan van Sertima so eloquently pointed out, Africans were the first people not only in Asia and Europe, but they had a major hand in building the Americas.[22] Finds discovered in New York City reveal that Africans were the early builders and farmers of New Amsterdam, the Dutch colonial name for New York. Skeletons of 427 Africans and hundreds of artifacts recovered from a burial ground beneath City Hall Park reveal how Africans played a major role in the building of New York City.[23] Once again, human remains that are natural signs, in other words, symptoms, are the deciding factors in analyzing historical events.

The educator, writer and diplomat James Weldon Johnson expressed his love for New York in a moving sonnet that showed that the symptomatic senses are indeed the most important and

---

[22] van Sertima, Ivan, **They Came Before Columbus: The African Presence in Ancient America**, Random House, New York (1976).

[23] Foerstel, Karen, New Black History Unearthed in City, *New York Post*, 8/4/97, p. 16.

compelling description that one can give for his inner emotions. Johnson states:

> When I come down to sleep death's endless night,
> The threshold of the unknown dark to cross,
> What to me then will be the keenest loss,
> When this bright world blurs on my fading sight?
> Will it be that no more I shall see the trees
> Or smell the flowers or hear the singing birds
> Or watch the flashing streams or patient herds?
> No, I am sure it will be none of these.
>
> But, ah! Manhattan's sights and sounds, her smells,
> Her crowds, her throbbing force, the thrill that comes
> From being of her a part, her subtle spells.
> Her shining towers, her avenues, her slums—
> O God! The stark, unutterable pity,
> To be dead, and never again behold my city! [24]

Johnson demonstrated that when one wants to get in touch with what is ultimate and the most meaningful in one's life, one must use a *Symptomatic Thought Process*. When one experiences beauty anywhere, one experiences it through natural signs, which of course are symptoms. A symbolic approach could never achieve such a result.

---

[24] Johnson, James Weldon, "My City", *Black Manhattan*, Da Capo Press, New York, 1930, pp. xv-xvi.

CONCLUSION

I realize the awesome change that will occur in civilization with the elimination of symbols, which have been around almost as long as humanity, and the introduction and implementation of the *Symptomatic Thought Process*. Every discipline on earth would be affected. Some of our most treasured beliefs would be eradicated because those beliefs are built on mythology. Despite the formidable metamorphoses that would take place, I cannot help but be extremely encouraged by what it would mean: the end of racism, mental illness, intertribal religious conflict, and the end of the greed and massacres that have occurred because of mythological assumptions held by different people of the world. The *Symptomatic Thought Process* must take place because humanity has no other choice.

While watching CNN, I saw the story of a young girl killed in Ireland because she was Protestant. The anguish that her father went through was the kind of existential absurdity that cannot linger if civilization is to be truly human. Will it take an awesome tragic catastrophe for man to wake up? What will it take for people to realize that a radical change must occur in behavior for us to have a civilization? The title of Diop's last book is very appropriate: *Civilization or Barbarism?*[1] Will we indeed have a civilization or will we have a barbaric world?

The current thinking is that we cannot rid the world of symbols or myth -- that we must have racism, religious wars, intertribal massacres and conflict throughout the world. This is unacceptable. The system that causes symbolic behavior must be

---

[1] Diop, Cheikh Anta, *Civilization or Barbarism: An Authentic Anthropology*, Lawrence Hill Books, Chicago (1991).

eradicated for us to make the decisions and initiate the behavior necessary for the world to survive in peace.

In the African community worldwide, we especially have a mandate to work together harmoniously whether on the continent or in the diaspora. We do not have to agree with each other, but we must work together out of love and respect for the common cause of total African liberation all over the globe. We cannot allow our egos to be our marching orders. We must stop seeing one another with defeatist attitudes. We must look at our fellow Africans with the respect that they deserve.

As Africans, our main problem is our inability to develop the kinds of relationships with each other that would enable us to work harmoniously together. This will never happen if we continue with our symbolic relationships -- that is, relationships built on myth. That creates a phony people that develop artificial relationships. That has not only been our problem, of course, but the problem with the whole of humanity. We cannot do business based on plastic, phony relationships. Relationships are the key, because they are more valuable than currency. In fact, relationships turn into currency.

The founders of re-engineering are now emphasizing process engineering, the manipulation, changing, and re-arranging of metaphors. We say that the only process change can be the elimination of metaphors and the symbolic thinking that produces metaphors. This comes about through the *Symptomatic Thought Process*. As of now - there is no concept operating in the world that does what is needed like the *Symptomatic Thought Process*. As humans begin new ways of looking at each other, new ideas and concepts will come into play. I firmly believe that the *Symptomatic Thought Process* will eventually solve the world's problems, as we know them.

In the United States, people are tired of the politics of symbolism. E. J. Dionne, Jr. stated in the *Washington Post*, in discussing the problems faced by Zoe Baird and Judge Kimba Wood with President Clinton during their nomination process:

Mostly, we've been remarkably inventive, and I sure
don't want us to spend our time trying to recreate the
world of three decades ago. But these are wrenching
issues, and Zoe Baird, Judge Wood (and, for that matter
Hillary Clinton) become convenient not as real human
beings but as symbols.

But if you want to understand why it was so easy for
the Clinton staff to see political equivalence between Zoe
Baird and Kimba Wood, here's part of the answer: it's
because we spend so much time using people as symbols
and symbols as a substitute for honest argument.[2]

This is a perfect example of the dynamics of symbolism and what
it does. We have turned people into symbols.

While Clinton was busy pontificating and using his symbols, in
an earlier scenario Gov. L. Douglas Wilder used a symptomatic
method to carry out justice. As noted in the *Richmond Times-
Dispatch*:

Gov. L. Douglas Wilder, fearing a 'miscarriage of
justice,' yesterday pardoned and ordered the immediate
release of an inmate who had been imprisoned almost
seven years on a conviction of raping a neighbor in
Alexandria.

The governor explained that tests of the DNA, or
genetic material, left on the victim raised serious doubts
about the guilt of Walter T. Snyder, Jr. Snyder's lawyers,
joined by Alexandria's chief prosecutor, had sought his
freedom.

'DNA evidence that has only recently come to light
contradicts   the   strong   case   that   was   ably
prosecuted...and decided by a jury during the trial in
June of 1986,' Wilder said. Just hours after Wilder's
action, Snyder, 27, dressed in a black T-shirt and jams
[sic], walked out of Nottoway Correctional Center into

---

[2] Dionne, E.J., Jr., *Washington Post*, 2/9/93.

the arms of his family and fiancee. He immediately thanked the governor for the pardon, said he felt no bitterness and said God had gotten him through the past seven years.[3]

Gov. Wilder used DNA, or genetic material, to properly liberate a man who was convicted wrongly. Gov. Wilder used a symptomatic method -- the symptoms being the DNA genetic material -- which proved beyond a doubt to be correct. Before the DNA came into question, the decision that put Walter Snyder in prison was based on myth. His conviction was based on mythological evidence produced by a symbolic thought process. (In recent years we have seen a proliferation of reversals of prison convictons due to DNA evidence.) This shows the necessity of thinking symptomatically if we are to even begin to carry out justice for all people.

Meanwhile, Gov. George Allen operated at the height of symbolism. The same *Richmond Times-Dispatch* stated:

> Democrats, some Republicans and state worker groups accused Gov. George Allen yesterday of putting symbolism ahead of substance by restricting taxpayer-financed abortions for government employees.
>
> 'I think he is trying to make a statement about his political beliefs and is putting state employees in a position they don't belong in – the middle of a political issue,' said Joan S. Dent, executive director of the 18,000-member Virginia Governmental Employees Association.
>
> Allen terminated unlimited abortion coverage for state employees under KeyAdvantage and other government-supplied health insurance policies. Effective July 1, insurance will pay for abortions under only three

[3] Hardy, Michael and Ruff, Jamie C., Wilder Pardons Rape-Case Inmate, *Richmond Times-Dispatch*, date unknown.

conditions: gross fetal deformity, rape or incest, or to save a woman's life.

Allen's move to cut abortion coverage was viewed as another overture to social and religious conservatives who dominate the GOP and who may look to Oliver L. North as an alternative to Allen for the U.S. Senate nomination in 2000.[4]

Those three examples clearly show Clinton and Allen using symbols and behaving symbolically; sandwiched in between is Gov. Wilder behaving symptomatically.

A *Financial Times* article on a conference of members of the Association of Southeast Asian Nations (ASEAN) shows the continuing attempt of Malaysia to do away with the mythological symbolism that produced rituals. The article states:

> The nine members of the Association of Southeast Asian Nations (ASEAN) hold their post-ministerial conference in Kuala Lumpur. Members put pageantry aside and sit down with 'dialogue partners' - including the US and EU - to discuss regional security Issues behind closed doors. As a result, it is seen as one of the most meaningful contacts between Southeast Asian powers and the rest of the world in the diplomatic calendar. The other dialogue partners are Canada, Japan, China, South Korea, Australia, New Zealand, India and Pakistan. Issues are likely to include the admission last week of Burma and Laos into the ASEAN grouping, as well as ASEAN's hope to turn Southeast Asia into a nuclear weapons-free zone. Madeleine Albright, the US secretary of state, is representing the U.S.[5]

By eradicating the pageantry and rituals, ASEAN members

---

[4] Schapiro, Jeff E. and Hardy, Michael, Allen Is Accused of Symbolism Over Substance, *Richmond Times-Dispatch*, 6/6/96.

[5] *Financial Times*, Weekly Calendar, 7/28/97.

got down to serious business to work on the problems at hand. They realized that the symbolism within the rituals does not play a part and is only a hindrance in dealmaking.

The view of the majority is to change metaphors and manipulate symbols -- that is, to reengineer. R. T. Rundle Clark states about the ancient Egyptians:

> "They manipulated the symbols of their myths to express their growing and earnest concern with the major problems of life. . . Myth is here passing into metaphor."[6]

This statement is ironic because it describes how the diffusion of myths and symbols occurred as people dealt with their most urgent issues. Clark describes how myth is metaphor and how the symbol system of metaphor is the dominant concept in ancient Egyptian thought. It is the same in the thinking of modern man. The manipulation of mythology to solve today's problems is rampant. That is why pressing problems are not being solved or even addressed properly.

---

[6] Clark , R. T. Rundle, *Myth and Symbol in Ancient Egypt,* Thames and Hudson, London, 1959, pp. 47 and 87.

AFTERWORD

As an ongoing component of my consulting work, I delivered a paper on Best Practices to a conference held by the National Productivity Corporation in Kuala Lumpur, Malaysia. Best Practices is a concept that is used practically by every major corporation in the world, yet its symbolic and mythological content is not readily acknowledged by its practitioners. Those dynamics are extremely important to understand, given the popularity of Best Practices. In my paper, I analyzed how the concept of Best Practices is used to spread mythology via symbolism to create an atmosphere of "business as usual". Following is my paper on Best Practices, as I delivered it in Kuala Lumpur:

BEST PRACTICES
Just a slogan? or a Catalyst for Productivity?

Copyright Edgar J. Ridley© 2000

The world's Western business community is very adept at manipulating mythological symbols that present themselves as metaphors for change. Such is what has happened with the slogan called Best Practices. Best Practices, which was popularized by Jack Welch of General Electric, is supposed to glean the best strategies for change and productivity from various management concepts such as re-engineering, process engineering, and a slew of strategic planning theories that are perpetuated by academicians. If one is familiar with the gyrations of Tom Peters and other would-be gurus, one knows that there is no end to the manipulation and changing of metaphors.

What does it mean to extract strategies from various concepts and adapt them to individual situations for productivity improvement? It simply means that metaphors intended for productivity improvement are manipulated, renamed, packaged and placed on the market for business consumption. These so-called Best Practices do not usher in qualitative change - it is really business as usual. In other words, the mythologies remain the same. Best Practices are built upon the prevailing mythologies built into the system vis - à-vis a symbol system that is all-pervasive in every area of human activity. It is impossible for any concept that is built on symbol systems to usher in qualitative change.

Granted, there has been excellent marketing of these concepts. Additionally, the world business community has been exceedingly gullible in adopting these concepts with the hopes that their firms will be liberated from impending financial doom. However, it should be understood that what is being marketed is a manipulation of metaphors. The traditional way of doing business is being maintained - the companies of industrialized nations have continued an attitude of wealth, a non-sharing behavior pattern, towards the so-called developing world. Best Practices is simply a method of maintaining superiority over companies in the so-called developing world.

The universal process used in Best Practices is very narrow and elitist. Best Practices refuses to deal with the dynamics of the real world such as racism, sexism and religion. As a result, Best Practices cannot create an arena of true justice and fairness.

For example, the solutions to problem-solving proposed by Best Practices are practically identical to the solutions found in Tom Peters' *In Search of Excellence* as well as all of the re-engineering and process engineering books. Unfortunately, Best Practice proponents just mimic the solutions to each other's problems. In short, the core dynamics that have been operative from the beginning of the quality movement haven't really changed qualitatively, not- withstanding the different spins put on them. The problem with these spins is that, linguistically, the metaphors change at a very rapid pace. That is due to our failure to realize that the neurological processes that produce symbolic behavior must be recognized, addressed and eliminated. It is unfortunate that the basic assumption held by behavioral specialists is that symbolic thinking is the norm. This common assumption concludes that the metaphors that derive from mythological thinking are essential, and any other process is a deviation from what is considered the norm. This basic assumption is the root cause of the problems that cause dysfunction in not only business but all areas of people activity.

What I propose is that when Homo sapiens began to think symbolically, that event was indeed a neurological mis-adventure. That thinking process produced mythology and superstition, which ushered in a type of behavior known as symbolic behavior. This was the beginning of man's making his most important personal and business decisions from a symbolic, or mythological, frame of reference. That phenomenon, which occurred in early history, has caused the type of business decisions and practices that we are addressing in today's world.

I am not alone in saying that symbolism produced a neurological misadventure. Prof. Max Müller suggested from his Chair at Oxford University, that,

> "Mythology is a disease of language. Ancient symbolism was a result of something like a primitive mental aberration. We know that mythology is the disease which springs up at a peculiar stage in human culture."[1]

What has to happen for this phenomenon to be corrected is that a *Symptomatic Thought Process®* must replace a symbolic thought process. This, interestingly, reverses assumptions and causes many academic feathers to fly. In Freudian and Jungian psychology, symptoms, by various degrees, were always inferior to symbols. Especially in Jungian psychology, if creativity is to take place, symptoms always turn into symbols. The research being done by Terrence Deacon at Harvard Medical School and Hospital[2] focuses on how symbol systems affect the neurological processes of the human brain. All scholars agree that the symptomatic thought process was first, and then out of that symptomatic process,

---

[1] Müller, Max, as quoted in Gerald Massey's Lectures, A&B Book Pubishers, New York, originally published 1900, p. 165.

[2] Deacon, Terrence W., *The Symbolic Species: The Co-evolution of Language and the Brain*, W.W. Norton & Co., New York, 1997.

the symbolic mode of thinking arose. This is what I call the neurological misadventure of primordial man.[3]

Typically, symptoms are thought of primarily to do with one's mental or physical health. However, recently, Harvard professor Marjorie Garber gave a non-medical spin to symptoms as she described how symptoms behave culturally:

> One of the most striking symptoms of culture in our time has been the phenomenon of the so-called cultural wars - a conflict that might be located precisely in the clash between the timeless function of the symbol and the historical function of the symptom.[4]

> We should look for a theory of the symptom, especially symptoms of culture."[5]

I stated in my book, *An African Answer: The Key to Global Productivity*, that

> "Symptomatic thinking will enable man to make the most effective business and personal decisions in any given situation in which man finds himself. It is indeed the key to the problems that face mankind."[6]

Indeed, Garber echoes my thesis, wherein I stated that the problems that we face in civilization are only to be solved between the dynamics of symbols and symptoms.[7] While Garber really doesn't go that far, she certainly suggests that it is the cause of the cultural wars that we face worldwide.

The same dynamics that cause these cultural wars affect businesses, simply because businesses can never remain isolated from the events around them. Businesses do not

[3] Ridley, Edgar ., J. *The Neurological Misadventure of Primordial Man*, published in <u>Black Male Female Relationships,</u> 1982.

[4] Garber, Marjorie, *Symptoms of Culture*, Routledge, New York, 1998, p. 7.

[5] Ibid., p. 9.

[6] Ridley, Edgar J., *An African Answer: The Key to Global Productivity*, Africa World Press, 1992, p. 32.

[7] Ibid., Ridley, Edgar J.

operate in isolation from the rest of society. That is the root problem that all these management slogans engender. They only operate on a very minute, superficial level that allows the so-called management status quo to feel comfortable in their individual ivory towers, while the illusion of success and high productivity rings in their ears.

Re-engineering is the perfect paradigm to this analysis. In its beginning, re-engineering was thought to be a real panacea. Corporations and businesses worldwide boarded the re-engineering bandwagon. Then re-engineering's creators, after reaping millions of dollars in fees, decided it didn't really work that well despite the fanfare and hoopla suggesting the opposite. The same hype is attached to Best Practices, which really should be titled Best Ways to Confuse and Go about Business as Usual.

What do I mean when I say business as usual? The business world still hides its head in the sand when dealing with racism. Instead, the best the business world can develop is an extremely weak agenda called multiculturalism. There is a real fear when dealing with the true issues that affect our lives. There is an avoidance of the hard choices and facts that would solve the cultural problems that are inherent in the new globalization that is presently taking place. For instance, a recent article in the New York Times titled *"Do Races Differ? Not Really DNA Shows"*, gives clear scientific evidence that correctly depicts the historical scenario of how the so-called races evolved. The article states:

> "We all evolved in the last 100,000 years from the same small number of tribes that migrated out of Africa and colonized the world."[8]

The article continues:

> "Modern Homo sapiens originated in Africa 200,000 to 1,000,000 years ago, at which point a relatively small number of them, maybe 10,000 or so,

---

[8] Dr. Craig J. Venter, head, Celera Genomics Corp., in "Do Races Differ? Not Really DNA Shows", New York Times, August 22, 2000.

began migrating into the Middle East, Europe, Asia and across the Bering land mass into the Americas". [9]

And finally:

"If you ask what percentage of your genes are reflected in your external appearance, the basis by which we talk about race, the answer would be in the range of .01 percent." [10]

We all came from Africa. There is only one race, the human race. That race is African. This is a scientific fact that should be known; there is no getting away from it. To rebuke these scientific findings is to be unable to face reality. Business is ineffective when the vast majority of people of colour are denied a share in operations and profits. Best Practices does not touch on the new anthropological and archaeological findings offered by genetics. These findings help change the way we feel about those who do not look like us. Unfortunately, the penchant for historical distortion and the tendency to hide historical truth is still prevalent throughout academia and the business community worldwide. This has not been dealt with, and so-called Best Practices ignores it. However, Best Practices could do nothing else, because as I stated before, it is business as usual. In our business schools, the most important and relevant courses such as Organizational Behavior and Business Policy are subordinated to finance courses. This is because the behavioral sciences, when taught properly, emphasize the behavior of people and how they make decisions that affect the currency around the world. If Best Practices proponents were sincerely interested in what is really best, this would mean a different way of doing business that is all-inclusive instead of exclusive.

As stated before, business as usual is manipulating and changing symbol systems that create myth and metaphors.

---

[9] Angier, Natalie, "Do Races Differ? Not Really DNA Shows", New York Times, August 22, 2000.

[10] Dr. Harold P. Freeman, Chief Executive, President, Directory of Surgery, North General Hospital, Manhattan, in "Do Races Differ? Not Really DNA Shows", New York Times, August 22, 2000.

This further confuses and suppresses historical truth and does not allow a fair and just civilization to emerge.

The alternative for best practices is the same alternative to all the ineffective management concepts that have been on the market. It is essential that we eradicate symbolic behavior and mythological thinking and replace it with a *Symptomatic Thought Process*®. Productivity would take on a whole new meaning because racism will be eliminated and the best minds will be at work. The people who are stifled and held back because of racism will be able to reach their potential. That can only come about through a civilization that is free of myth. Marjorie Garber, in her book, *Symptoms of Culture*, suggested that we must look for a theory of the symptom. This is exactly what Edgar J Ridley & Associates has accomplished with the *Symptomatic Thought Process*®, a concept that radically rearranges the structure of civilization as never before.

I was invited to lecture and participate in a conference on productivity and the workforce in the 21st century in Shanghai, China. The conference was attended by business leaders and scholars from all over Asia.

My paper was entitled *Productivity in the 21st Century*, and a brief excerpt follows:

PRODUCTIVITY IN THE 21ST CENTURY

The late W. Edwards Deming emphasized in his book, **Out of the Crisis**, that quality need not suffer in the wake of productivity nor should productivity suffer in the wake of quality. Indeed, if productivity is to take place, there has to be matching quality. If economic stability is to be achieved in the 21st century, the global workforce has to be armed with a new mandate.

The problems that the world community has faced in this past decade are very apparent. Europe and the West have had to face the economic boom in the Pacific Rim. The fact is that economic power has truly shifted from Europe and the West to Asia.

There have been various concepts put forth by management consultants and theorists to achieve global productivity. One of these concepts is called Reengineering, which was created by two United States consultants and has enjoyed a degree of worldwide appeal, especially in Europe. Reengineering is simply the changing of operational metaphors and redoing strategies that have been in place to insure maximum efficiency. Unfortunately, although Western corporations and businesses have spent millions on reengineering projects, reengineering has proven to have serious shortcomings: it has resulted in layoffs, and has actually failed to deliver its promises of enhanced quality and productivity. In fact, its creators have admitted its failures, and are now emphasizing the **process** aspect of reengineering.

What many scholars have failed to recognize is that as we enter the 21st Century the workforce will not be adequate no matter what their training, unless they understand the dynamics of symbolism and the resulting metaphors and superstitions that result from symbolic activity. Metaphors and myths are synonymous. What is symbolic is anything which implies something more than its obvious and immediate meaning. In other words, a symbol is that which possesses specific connotations in addition to its conventional and obvious meaning. A symbol implies something vague or unknown or hidden from us.[11] Scholars throughout the world have traditionally thought of symbols as a necessity of human thought. This is not true. Symbols and symbolic behavior are counterproductive and have caused distress in the workforce for centuries.

The global workforce and management must realize that if economic stability is to be achieved in the 21st Century, there has to be a radical change in the way we do business. That radical change is the discarding of symbols and symbolic behavior, which means the discarding of decisions based on metaphor or myth.

Symbols, which have their origin in Africa, have been used throughout the world. However, Africans have used symbols and symbolic behavior in a very aggressive way and this has resulted in symbolic behavior that has been entrenched in mythology, superstition, and ritual. That has also been the case with Asia, Europe, and Latin America but to a lesser extent. Where you have heavily entrenched symbolism

---

[11] Jung, Carl G., *Man and His Symbols*.

and mythology, you have severe conditions of poverty, non-productive behavior, and an inability to make decisions based on reality.

It must be emphasized that the economic and cultural conflicts around the world are conflicts based on **symbolism** and the **acting out of its mythology.** You will find that in Africa with the conflicts in Rwanda and Zaire; in Europe with the conflicts in Ireland between the Protestants and Catholics; and throughout Asia with the conflicts between different religious and ethnic factions. These conflicts will persist and increase in severity unless we rid ourselves of symbolism and its ongoing mythologies. In fact, racism is a result of mythological thinking, and the West uses that myth to try to continue its worldwide domination. The West is very nervous about China and its great economic potential. Countries that have people of color pose a great threat to the white economic populace, who have been accustomed to having complete economic control of the world.

That is why it is extremely important for China and the rest of Asia to realize that it **must form strong links** with geographical areas like Africa. That is indeed the West's worst nightmare. Joint ventures have already been formed at a high rate between countries like Malaysia and Zimbabwe, and numerous other Asian countries are involved in economic ventures throughout the continent of Africa. This is an exciting phase of global business transactions, for it combats the various European economic blocs. One cannot avoid the issues of racism and religious conflicts, for they impede productivity around the world and have a severe effect on economic stability that continues to bewilder and perplex the world's top economists. This refusal to deal with these sensitive issues continues to raise havoc on the world economy. In the United States, these issues are so sensitive that in some quarters it is forbidden to discuss them. That is why the United States and Europe are in such a great state of denial. And this is why it is so important for China and the rest of Asia, and indeed, Africa, to understand the dynamics of symbolism and its resulting mythology.

In my book, **An African Answer,** I describe the phenomenon of symbolism and its resulting effects and what has to take place for that symbolism and symbolic behavior to be eliminated. What I have proposed is a Symptomatic

Thought Process in place of the symbolic thought process. I
will give a short elaboration of my theory.

When the Western scholars Freud and Jung reached their
conclusions on the behavior of people the world over, they
balanced the dynamics of symbolism and symptoms. It has
been generally accepted that symbolism and symbolic
behavior take precedence over symptoms and all other entities.
This was particularly the conclusion of the physician, Carl
Jung. Symbols are always a complete **substitute** for what is
real. They have **no connection whatsoever**, physical or
otherwise, to what is real. On the other hand, symptoms have a
real and paramount connection to all things that are real.
Indeed, symptoms are a natural outgrowth of not only what is
real, but also a necessary connection to the realities of the
universe in a way that symbols can never be.

For instance, we know that if you have a cold, you will
have a runny nose, perhaps watery eyes, and a cough. These
are considered **symptoms** of a cold. Symptoms are a natural
and normal process. Symbols lack that process and therefore
must be discarded. Symbols have no useful service in the
issues of productivity, quality, and anything that can make
civilization just and productive. This is a complete reversal of
what has been taught and practiced for millennium.

For China to continue its great economic growth, we must
find ways to understand the destruction that symbolism has
caused and its resulting mythology. If we are to understand
the behavior of people the world over, we have to understand
the dynamics and phenomenon of symbolism.

People in various areas of the world do not understand the
phenomenon of symbolism and its impact on their everyday
life. In my book, **An African Answer: The Key to Global
Productivity**, I explain the dynamics of symbolism and
mythology. Improvements must be made. It is imperative for
those people who are in charge of human resources to
comprehend the destructive nature of symbolism and its
ensuing result: the making of decisions based on myth.

I realize that this will be an arduous task, for it means
changing attitudes that we've held for so long. However, no
other theories or management concepts have worked. If we
continue on this path of conflict, disrespect for, and
intolerance of other groups who are different from us, we will
be headed toward global barbarism and destruction. We have

to realize that basically we are all the same, and the top anthropologists in the world have verified that. It is clearly understood that human life began in Africa and spread throughout the entire world. With that diffusion of ideas and concepts, Africans and Asians must seek closer ties. We must destroy the myths of the world that keep people apart and cause conflict and destruction.

My remarks were favorably received by the Chinese but were greeted with hostility by the white participants. The whites seemed to be constantly in a state of fear and insecurity, as if paralyzed by the statement of Pliny the Elder: "There is always something new out of Africa."

In 1980, I wrote *The Neurological Misadventure of Primordial Man*. My thesis was that Homo sapiens suffered a neurological misadventure the moment he began to symbolize and mythologize. The paper was originally published in *The Journal of Black Male/Female Relationships* by publisher Nathan Hare. It was then republished by the *National Newport News & Commentator*, by H. Khalifah. I presented my thesis to Dr. Cheikh Anta Diop at the Radiocarbon Laboratory at the University of Dakar, Senegal (now known as the University of Cheikh Anta Diop). My thesis states:

THE NEUROLOGICAL MISADVENTURE OF PRIMORDIAL MAN

In Chancellor Williams' classic work, *The Destruction of Black Civilization*, he raises the paramount question, "What happened to a people who built the pyramids, who now live in the projects?" The works of Cheikh Anta Diop, George G. M. James, Yosef ben-Jochannan, John G. Jackson, and John Henrik Clarke all have stimulated more research into the depth of the enslavement of African people. These scholars spent their entire lives and sacrificed much to bring the true history of African people to the masses of Black people the world over. They have corrected the distortions of those academicians who have attempted to disgrace and distort the history of African people in the homeland and the diaspora.

However, Professor Williams' question has yet to be answered. What happened to a people who created most, if not all, of what is used in today's highly technological civilization? African people, who were the first family, created the technology that so-called white, or Caucasian, people use today to enhance their control over the world's majority.

We are at a point now where it is not enough to deal solely with the great achievements of African people in antiquity and the so-called Golden Age, where Black people had not only the first civilization, but flourished the world over. What is of utmost importance now is the fact that while historically, we were once on top, we are now on the bottom and continue to function as if that is the norm.

We will maintain here that African people, who were the first people to create symbols and symbolic behavior, produced an abundance, and indeed, an overabundance, of rituals and superstitions, which led to their downfall. Subsequently, Arabs and later on white Europeans came in and destroyed these African people and their culture, and that destruction is continuing as we live today.

There are numerous definitions of the word symbol. However, the best working definition is a neurological one. Despite current opinion among scholars that symbols can mean different things to different people, and that a clear-cut definition of symbols is difficult to obtain, it should be made clear here that a symbol is nothing but a representation of the real thing. A symbol is a mental representation of reality. In other words, a symbol is a substitute. A symbol, because it is a substitute, is a plastic entity. It is not real within itself, but a representation. It can be mental (neurological), or an entity that is physical and long-standing, having undergone various stages in its growth.

Traditionally, symbols have been thought to be a natural process of brain function and brain development. Traditionally, symbols have been perceived to be a natural process of the dynamics of culture. It has been traditionally held by theologians and anthropologists that spirituality or spiritual forces produced symbols, which resulted in rituals and ceremonies. This view, indeed, is held by historians and anthropologists in relation to African culture, where there was a great deal of ritualistic activity that evolved from the so-called religious experience of primordial man. Scholar after scholar has dealt with the symbolic input of people and their culture and the traditional assumption has been that symbols are a natural ingredient and process of man.

Norman O. Brown makes the statement, "The axis on which world history turns is symbolism. "[12] John Dewey has boldly said that the discovery of symbols has been the greatest single achievement in world history. White scholars from one end of the earth to the other have undertaken the study of symbolism as an isolated entity. Symbols and symbolism are the most important ingredients that exist in the world today. They motivate behavior from birth to death. Psychiatric physicians Karl Jung and Sigmund Freud did monumental studies on the function of symbolism as it relates to human behavior and its importance in the study of mental illness. Both Freud and Jung exposed the telltale signs of symbols as they gave clues to the mental health of psychiatric patients, as well as people who are classified as mentally healthy.

Psychologist Arthur Janov, who is well known for his works involving primal therapy, further implemented the works of Freud and Jung. However, Janov departed from Jung and Freud, by pinpointing and emphasizing the destructive capabilities of "inappropriate symbolism."[13] Janov defines mental illness as inappropriate symbolism. In other words, Janov posits that when we act out past destructive experiences, usually from our childhood, we act out these past experiences symbolically. In doing so, we fail to match the symbol to the appropriate symptom. Janov concludes by stating that good mental health is matching the symbol to the correct pain. Janov, who worked with neurologist Michael Holden, documented the fact that inappropriate symbolism, or symbolic behavior, is the cause of most mental illness in American society.

Unfortunately, while Janov emphasized the destructive nature of symbolism, he opts for appropriate symbolism as a cure. In other words, Janov states that while mental illness is inappropriate symbolism, symbolism is a normal function of the brain process as it reacts to outside stimuli. Janov sanctions

---

[12] Brown, Norman O., *Love's Body*, University of California Press, 1966, p. 215.

[13] Janov, Arthur, Ph.D. and Holden, E. Michael, M.D., *Primal Man: The New Consciousness*, Thomas Y. Crowell Co., New York (1975).

the function of symbolism when it matches the correct, or core point, of our beginning.

Janov is one of the few people who has identified symbols as the cause of most of the major problems that we face in a highly technological society. But Janov, who received his cue from Freud and Jung, fails to see the necessity to eradicate all symbols from the human psyche. He is superb in identifying the dynamics of symbolism as it functions in primordial man. He states:

> Neurosis filled the bill. It allowed killing to become an acceptable part of living, and those who could not do so were the least fit to survive. In this way, it was the neurotics who survived. Feelings could be transmuted into symbolic form; the elaborateness of the ritualistic and symbolic life being commensurate with the amount of loss of self. . . Man could then kill for his symbols. He could eliminate others to please the gods or murder for religious reasons. He could kill others when the state (flag) and a structure, not himself, was threatened.[14]

African people were the creators of the first symbol. In fact, the Twa people created the first symbol that we know of. European nomenclature refers to these early people as pygmies. These Twa people felt the need to express their spirituality symbolically; hence, their first symbol was a religious one.

Going back as far as we can theologically, from the first theological system, which was an African mythological system, to the latest theological thought in use today, symbols were thought to be a natural ingredient of one's specific spiritual experience. Symbols are believed to be a natural outgrowth and result of one's spirituality.

I maintain that this has been one of the great errors of civilization. This is the core reason why all religions have failed to be a catalyst for peace, liberation and justice throughout the whole of civilization. The Egyptologist Gerald Massey explored symbolism in his monumental volumes, *The Book of the*

---

[14] Janov, Arthur, Ph.D. and Holden, E. Michael, M.D., ibid., p. 18.

Beginnings. Massey's research started with early man in Africa, all the way to late Christianity. Massey suggested that all religions, by virtue of their symbolic intent, would have to be re-evaluated for their distortion, due to the implicit and prevalent symbolic ingredient in all of the world religions. Massey, who wrote his works over 100 years ago, was the first to explore the symbolic distortions and references in the world's major religions.

To say that symbolism is an outgrowth of spirituality is a misdemeanor, and should be very clear to the intelligent mind. One must realize that one's spirituality, or what one experiences from various entities in one's life is originally real, but in order for that realness to make an impact, it must remain real in its qualitativeness. Hence, a symbolic inference can never retain the authenticity of that original entity, because once it becomes symbolic it loses all originality and qualitativeness. We must remember that all symbols are substitutes.

Once Black people have the understanding of what a symbol really is, there can be no confusion as to what is real and what is symbolic.

With all due respect for traditional thought patterns about African cultures and the beauty and necessity of its rituals, ceremonies, and superstitions as a necessary ingredient to the growth of African people, I maintain that this has not been the case. I know this will be very hard for most of us to accept. However, the fact is that the rituals and superstitions of African people that emanated from the so-called spiritual experience, once that experience became symbolic, lost all of their original qualitative power. Therefore, these rituals and superstitions lost all facsimile of being a liberating force for the growth, spirituality, and power of all African people.

It is beyond my comprehension why Black people continue to opt for and be fooled by symbols. Black people fail to understand the difference between symbols and substance. Black people fail to realize that symbols and reality are indeed opposite. Black people fail to understand that "symbols (are) essentially plastic." [15]

---

[15] Berryman, Phillip E., *Latin American Liberation Theology*, in **Theology in the Americas**, edited by Sergio Torres and John Eagleson, Orbis Books, New York (1976), p. 43.

I'd like to explain the difference between symbols and signs. Traditionally, it has been held that symbols are of greater importance than signs, and indeed, the difference between signs and symbols is not important. Once again, traditional academia has been wrong, and tragically so.

Susanne Langer, in her interesting book, *Philosophy in a New Key*, has the best definition of signs and symbols. She states:

> A sign indicates the existence, past, present and future, of a thing, event, or condition. Wet streets are a sign that it has rained. A smell of smoke signifies the presence of fire. . . . all examples here adduced are natural signs. A natural sign is a part of a greater event or of a complex condition, and to an expert observer, it signifies the rest of that situation of which it is a *notable feature. It is a symptom of a state of affairs.* [16] [Emphasis mine].

Langer is saying that the paramount difference between a sign and a symbol is that a sign can have the original ingredient of that to which it points. However, a symbol cannot have the original ingredient, and is always a complete substitute. A symbol is always a complete, plastic entity. Taking that bit of information into consideration, it is a natural process of intelligent thought that the entity that springs qualitatively from spirituality, or ultimate reality, must be a significant part of the vibrations that are transferable from that original entity. In other words, a symbol can never be a viable factor in one's experience, due to the fact that it lacks qualitative originality. A sign, by virtue of it being a natural sign, can have the original ingredient from whence it originated.

The equation that must operate in a neurological vein must be ultimate reality (which is the genesis of everything)	= Symptoms (natural signs)	= Ultimate reality

[16] Langer , Susanne K., *Philosophy in a New Key: A Study in the Symbolism of Reason, Rite and Art,* Mentor Books, New York (1948), pp. 94-95.

This equation must be understood and adopted if African people are ever to retake the world and overthrow white dominance.

Now it might be asked: if symbolism destroyed African people, and was a core point in the destruction of African civilization, then why didn't it do the same to white civilizations? It must be made very clear that African people were the first people on this planet Earth. It also must be understood that no people on the face of this earth were steeped in symbolism to the extent of African people. Our highly ritualistic behavior and traditions can prove that. The strong ritualistic and superstitious nature of African people need hardly be disputed. While our rituals and ceremonies may be entertaining to look at, and indeed fun to participate in, they had no meaningful interplay in our relationships, our power to defend ourselves, or our ability to engage in real truthfulness and harmony with each other. I maintain that our ritualistic and superstitious behavior played a significant part in our downfall. How were Europeans able to return to Africa, after migrating northward, and exploit African people to the extent that they did? I maintain that Europeans learned the difference between symbols and substance. They mastered the manipulation of symbols to the degree that they were able to manipulate African people into a state of servitude that exists until today. How did they accomplish this?

The Sacred Signs and Symbols which were evolved by the Nilotic Negroes must be taken into consideration in our argument to show the origin and meaning of many which have been brought on in every Cult up to the present-day Christian Doctrines.

To comprehend why these were invented and used, we have to carry ourselves back into that early state of the evolution of the human race when man had no words to express all his ideas and beliefs. He had 'to think in things' which were visible before any abstract ideas were evolved in the human brain. Man observed nature in all its phases, which was ever before him visually; it was there objectively; there could be no imagination in the visible facts of nature or nature's Laws. Not possessing sufficient words, he objectified these powers by inventing signs and symbols which would best convey to his mind the powers of these elemental Spirits. Each sign or symbol typified the best image he was able to produce, objectively representing the qualities or properties, of a Spirit, or power, in nature's universe.

*The Dual God Horus-Set, or
The Black God and The White God.*

Naturally, the first two man would image would be Light and Darkness, Day and Night. Therefore the primary imagery of the first two Heroes representing the elementary powers of Light and Darkness, Night

and Day, were represented by two birds--ONE
WHITE, ONE BLACK--as two personal Totems
representing Horus and Set.[17] [Emphasis mine].

When Europeans returned to their original home, Africa,
Africans viewed Europeans as their myth coming into reality.

The two primary [powers] were twin-brothers, Set
and Horus, representing as powers, Night and Day, or
Darkness and Light, assigned as Set, God of the South,
and Horus, God of the North. . . [18]

Without doubt the contention of Set and Horus began with
the conflict of darkness and light, drought and water, when these
were elemental powers, and the birthplace of the twin brothers—
one Black and one Light--was in the bed of reeds. The phase
was continued in all the cults. In the Lunar, by the twins who
struggled for supremacy in the dark and light halves of the moon,
which yet imaged the light eye of Horus and the dark eye of Set.
But the war extended to the whole of nature that was divided in
halves betwixt the Set and Horus twins who were the firstborn of
the ancient Mother in two of her several characters.[19] [Emphasis
mine].

Africans looked upon Europeans as symbols, or
representations, of Horus (mental representations of reality). It
would be fair to suggest that because of the preference for day,
for light, African people worshipped Europeans, who, in their
physical likeness to light (white skin), represented a real-life
replica of Horus.

---

[17] Churchward, Albert, *Origin and Evolution of Religion*, George Allen & Unwin,
Ltd., London (1924), p. 67.

[18] Churchward, Albert, ibid., p. 19.

[19] Churchward, Albert, ibid., p.p. 62-63.

The following cartoon was featured in major metropolitan newspapers across the United States. It illustrates the way whites view Africans.

"With a little luck, they may revere us as gods."

***From The Far Side* by Gary Larson -**
Reprinted by permission of Chronicle Features, San Francisco, CA

I sympathize with those scholars and people who emphasize the great glory and the great heritage of African culture and tradition. But **we must be thoroughly honest**. We must realize that all rituals and superstition evolved out of symbolism. These entities have not freed African people on the continent or in the diaspora. We awaken daily as if it is the norm to be on the bottom the world over. The reality is that African people worldwide must be interested in their liberation now. We must not be content to just sit back and talk about a past glory that African people today are not experiencing. What matters to me, and I dare say the majority of Black people today, is our situation now, what our situation will be in the future, and the prospects of freedom. Being in chains today and talking about a glorious past will not do it. As a matter of fact, that is a weird kind of schizophrenia that has yet to be textbooked in the annals of mental health.

What is needed is a workable equation, not just an impotent, intellectual exercise that has no possibility of being a practical praxis for worldwide African liberation.

We should understand clearly the position of white people, or so-called Caucasians. Their position has been outlined succinctly by Frances Cress Welsing, who maintained that white people are genetic mutations from albinism, and they did indeed spring from African people. The theory that whites evolved from Africans has also been documented thoroughly by Cheikh Ante Diop in *The African Origins of Civilization: Myth or Reality*. It has also been documented by Egyptologists such as Gerald Massey in his volumes, *A Book of the Beginnings* and *Ancient Egypt*, as well as Albert Churchward in *The Origins and Evolution of the Human Race* and *Signs and Symbols of Primordial Man*. These scholars have diligently stated, as far back as a hundred years before modern anthropologists discovered any finds in Africa, that Blacks originated in Africa and migrated northward, and before 20,000 B.C., white people were not to be found. White people appeared on the scene some time after 20,000 B.C. We know that process to be one of genetic mutation. In terms of exact dates and times, we do not know. But we do know that because of Welsing's *Cress Theory of Color-Confrontation*, there has been a proliferation of genetic conferences held by whites around the world.

White people have a definite fear of genetic annihilation. This means that if white people do not discover a way to survive in a world where they are a real minority, they realize they face the real possibility of genetic annihilation. If we understand that, and realize the psychological and psychiatric dynamics behind that white fear, then we will not feel intimidated by white distortions of our historical process. In other words, we cannot allow white historical distortions and false superiority claims to destroy our ability and courage to look at our culture critically and honestly, as we struggle to make sense out of the real dilemma of continual Black enslavement the world over. A failure to do this will mean the complete genocide of African people. African people must not be afraid to introduce new theories and do independent research outside of the norm. Most Black scholars continue to function under the values and norm of white academia.

I realize that the proposition that symbolism, from a neurological starting point is a misadventure and must be abandoned, presupposes a thought pattern unheard of in world academia. However, I maintain that the mind process that crystallizes certain aspects of energy from our experiences and creates symbols is a brain misadventure that disallows any possibility of creativity, because the experiences that the brain crystallizes cannot be relayed with any kind of reality. The correct neurological adventure that takes place is that the brain crystallizes, if anything, natural signs from our experiences. These natural signs, or symptoms, create reality, or bits of reality, from ultimate reality, or from those experiences that are an original part of that core reality. I want to emphasize that the alternative to symbols and thinking symbolically is symptoms, or thinking symptomatically.

Ultimate reality is simply what one experiences ultimately. Nothing can be experienced more, qualitatively. In theological circles, it has been stated that one cannot experience ultimate reality. However, I maintain that if man cannot experience qualitatively what is ultimate, then all theological talk needs to cease. Any further talk of God, or one's ultimate spirit, is fruitless. It is a tragic mistake to assume that all peoples around the world cannot experience ultimate reality because of their different cultural experiences. It is a tragic mistake and a cop-out. What that really suggests is that Black people can never be free. And indeed, even though some of us wake up each morning as if being on the bottom in servitude to white people is the norm, using symbols in place of ultimate reality, or spiritual impulses, produces a very, very frictional people who are continually in a state of conflict, jealousy, and rivalry. I think that very well describes the picture of Black people today. We must admit that if we are serious about Black peoples' freedom around the world.

What I am stating here is that because African people around the world continue to refuse to act on and understand the difference between substance and symbols; because African people around the world choose to follow what is symbolic and plastic; they continue to be slaves to a white minority population. No amount of glorifying the so-called Golden Age, our creativity in antiquity, and our achievements in terms of the first civilization, will mean a thing. We have got to answer the question: if indeed we were so great, what happened? I say we were great. But any people that continually allow themselves to be led symbolically will disintegrate.

From the first Twa symbols, ✤ to the modern Christian Cross ✚ , we have been tricked.

So we ask: If psychologists are stating that symbols produce symbolic behavior, and we understand the entities that are involved in that symbolism, what are the results and the dynamics of the eradication of symbols in one's life? The symbolic ramifications are immense. Black people and the Black family are being destroyed the world over by drugs. Drugs (all drugs, including prescription drugs, particularly ones prescribed by psychiatric physicians) are substitutes that are prevalent in the behavior patterns of symbolic-behaving people. We must remember that psychologists are now documenting and offering proof that people behaving symbolically are indeed neurotic. That is what neurosis is: people who operate symbolically, or use inappropriate symbolism. When people are oppressed, and there is no struggle to free themselves, something must emerge as a substitute that can block the reality of that situation. Traditionally, alcohol, temporary hard drugs and so-called soft or proper (which are medically induced) drugs have been the substitute behind which people have hidden their reality, or masked their pain. Dr. Yosef ben-Jochannan is correct when he states that all drugs, including alcohol, are used primarily for the continual colonization of a people of color the world over.

Advertising has taken advantage of its sophisticated symbolism to manipulate the minds of millions of people to operate in a manner that upholds worldwide white supremacy. In the Black community, the advertising for Jacquin's liquor is "It is a vodka for prestige," while in the white community, "It is the toast of the town," The not-so-subtle implication is that for Black people, the buzzword is prestige--who can be the most prestigious, or in fact, who can show the most symbolic power. The powers of media manipulation, with their use of symbolism, continually enslave and castrate any strength in the Black community, and we continually succumb.

Even our uprisings, our so-called "riots," have been misdirected to symbolic targets. The march on Washington in the '60s was symbolic in nature, and utterly fruitless in terms of qualitative change. But Black people do not realize that. Once again, it took an Indian to call attention to the symbolic nature of the marches in the '60s. Vine Deloria, Jr., in *We Talk, You Listen*, described Martin Luther King as the master of symbolic activity, in his continual marches and demonstrations, that, when looked at honestly, were no catalyst for qualitative change at all.

I realize the difficulty of rearranging traditional thought patterns that have been in practice for hundreds of thousands of years. It cannot be emphasized too strongly that it is necessary for an equation to be **used and experienced**, rather than just read intellectually. I maintain that by the eradication of symbols, one forces oneself into a seeming abyss, where one can deal with nothing but ultimate reality, or reality. Then, we, as Black people, will initiate the kind of behavior that will be strongly pertinent in our freedom. We will not destroy other African leaders, yet allow South Africa to be controlled by white people. We will stop the intertribal conflict that we have grown used to. We will stop killing other Africans, and redirect our energies to those who are implicated in our real oppression.

Non-symbolic African man will cease to be fooled by symbolic manipulation. He will be able to deal with his experiences with a reality that can only come from seeing things symptomatically, rather than symbolically.

My theory that symbolism accounts for a neurological misadventure and we must think symptomatically has proven to be one of the most controversial concepts to have ever been created. It has been met with either a wall of silence or heated debate. The scientist and scholar Edward Whitmont advocates a pattern where we both live and think symptomatically and symbolically, and this seems to be the traditional way of seeing life patterns. For me, this allows for a paranoid, schizophrenic individual that accounts for the racism and mental illness that has produced a civilization that is truly barbaric in its basic nature. Only time will tell what is the correct way to proceed. I am totally convinced that the *Symptomatic Thought Process* is the only way out of our despair. The *Symptomatic Thought Process* will solve all of our problems.

SELECTED BIBLIOGRAPHY

Ani, Marimba, *Yurugu,* Africa World Press, Trenton (1994)

Ayittey, George B.N., *Africa Betrayed*, St. Martin's Press, New York (1992)

ben-Jochannan , Dr. Yosef A.A., *Black Man of the Nile and His Family*, Black Classic Press (1989)

Bell, Derrick, *Faces at the Bottom of the Well: The Permanence of Racism*, BasicBooks, New York (1992)

Bernal, Martin, *Black Athena: The Afroasiatic Roots of Classical Civilization – Volume II, The Archaeological and Documentary Evidence,* Rutgers University Press, New Brunswick (1991)

Berryman, Phillip E., Latin American Liberation Theology, in *Theology in the Americas*, Torres, Sergio and Eagleson, John, ed., Orbis Books, New York (1976)

Brown, Norman O., *Love's Body*, University of California Press (1966)

Campbell, Joseph, with Moyers, Bill, *The Power of Myth*, Doubleday (1988)

Cavalli-Sforza, L. Luca, M.D., Menozzi, Paolo, M.D., and Piazza, Alberto, M.D., *The History and Geography of Human Genes*, Princeton University Press, Princeton (1994)

Celenko, Theodore, *Egypt in Africa*, Indianapolis Museum of Art in cooperation with the Indiana University Press (1996)

Churchward, Albert, *Origin and Evolution of Religion*, George Allen & Unwin, Ltd., London (1924)

Churchward, Albert, *Signs and Symbols of Primordial Man*, George Allen & Co., Ltd., London (1913)

Clark, R. T. Rundle, *Myth and Symbol in Ancient Egypt*, Thames and Hudson, London (1959)

Cook, Scott D. N., Technological Revolutions and the Gutenberg Myth, *Internet Dreams: Archetypes, Myths and Metaphors*, Stefik, Mark, ed., Massachusetts Institute of Technology (1996)

Deacon, Terrence W., *The Symbolic Species: The Co-Evolution of Language and the Brain*, W.W. Norton & Co., New York (1997)

Deming, W. Edwards, *Out of the Crisis*, Massachusetts Institute of Technology, Center for Advanced Engineering Study, Cambridge (1982)

Diop, Cheikh Anta, *Civilization or Barbarism: An Authentic Anthropology*, Lawrence Hill Books, Chicago (1991)

Eliade, Images and Symbols, as quoted in Whitmont, Edward C., *The Symbolic Quest*, Princeton University Press, Princeton (1969)

Fraser, James G., *The Golden Bough: The Roots of Religion and Folklore*, Avenel Books, New York (1981)

Hacker, Andrew, *Two Nations: Black and White, Separate, Hostile, Unequal*, Charles Scribner's Sons, (1992)

Henderson, Joseph L., Ancient Myths and Modern Man, *Man and His Symbols*, Jung, Carl G., ed., Doubleday, New York (1964)

Herrnstein, Richard J. and Murray, Charles, *The Bell Curve: Intelligence and Class Structure in American Life*, The Free Press, New York (1995)

Janov, Arthur, Ph.D. and Holden, E. Michael, M.D., *Primal Man: The New Consciousness*, Thomas Y. Crowell Co., New York (1975)

Johnson, James Weldon, *Black Manhattan*, DaCapo Press, New York, (1930)

Jung, Carl G., Ed., *Man and His Symbols,* Doubleday, New York (1964)

Kast, Verena, *The Dynamics of Symbols: Fundamentals of Jungian Psychotherapy*, Fromm International, New York (1992)

King, Richard, M.D., The Symbolism of the Crown in Ancient Egypt, paper delivered at conference on Nile Valley Civilizations, Atlanta, September 1984.

Ki-Zerbo, J., Ed., *UNESCO, General History of Africa, Volume I - Methodology and African Prehistory*, James Currey Publishers, California (1989)

Langer , Susanne K., *Philosophy in a New Key: A Study in the Symbolism of Reason, Rite and Art,* Mentor Books, New York (1948)

Lefkowitz, Mary R. and Rogers, Guy MacLean, ed., *Black Athena Revisited,* University of North Carolina Press, Chapel Hill (1996)

Lewis, Reginald F. and Walker, Blair S., *Why Should White Guys Have All the Fun? How Reginald Lewis Created a Billion-Dollar Business Empire*, John Wiley & Sons, New York (1995)

Mandela, Nelson, Foreword, *The African Dream: Visions of Love and Sorrow: The Art of John Muafangejo*, Levinson, Orde, Thames and Hudson (1992)

Massey, Gerald, *Ancient Egypt: The Light of the World*, reprinted by Black Classic Press, Baltimore (1992)

Massey, Gerald, *A Book of the Beginnings: Concerning an Attempt to Recover and Reconstitute the Lost Origins of the Myths and Mysteries, Types and Symbols, Religion and Language, with Egypt for the Mouthpiece and Africa as the Birthplace,* Black Classic Press, Baltimore (1881, reprinted 1995)

Massey, Gerald, *The Natural Genesis: or Second Part of A Book of the Beginnings: Concerning an Attempt to Recover and Reconstitute the Lost Origins of the Myths and Mysteries, Types and Symbols, Religion and Language, with Egypt for the Mouthpiece and Africa as the Birthplace,* Black Classic Press, Baltimore (1881, reprinted 1995)

May, Rollo, *The Cry for Myth*, Dell Publishing, New York (1991)

Moss, Robert, *Death Beam*, Berkley Publishing Group, New York (1981)

Muafangejo, John *The African Dream: Visions of Love and Sorrow: The Art of John Muafangejo*, Levinson, Orde, Thames and Hudson (1992)

Peters, Thomas J. and Waterman, Robert H., Jr., *In Search of Excellence: Lessons From America's Best Run Companies*, Warner Books, New York (1982)

Peters, Thomas J., *Liberation Management: Necessary Disorganization for the Nanosecond Nineties*, Alfred A. Knopf, New York (1992)

Peters, Thomas J., *The Tom Peters Seminar: Crazy Times Call for Crazy Organizations*, Vintage Books, New York (1994)

Ridley, Edgar J., *An African Answer: The Key to Global Productivity*, Africa World Press, Trenton (1992)

Ridley, Edgar J., *The Neurological Misadventure of Primordial Man*, The National Newport News and Commentator, Newport News, VA

Sproul, Barbara C., *Primal Myths: Creation Myths Around the World*, HarperCollins, San Francisco (1991)

Stringer, Christopher and McKie, Robin, *An African Exodus: The Origins of Modern Humanity*, Henry Holt & Co., New York (1996)

Thurow, Lester, *Head to Head: The Coming Economic Battle Among Japan, Europe, and America* (1993)

Tillich, Paul, Symbols of Faith, *Religion From Tolstoy to Camus*, Kaufmann, Walter, ed., Harper & Row, New York (1961)

van Sertima, Ivan, **They Came Before Columbus: The African Presence in Ancient America**, Random House, New York (1976)

Walker, Alice, and Parmar, Pratibha, *Warrior Marks*, Harcourt Brace & Company, New York (1993)

Wee, Lee, Changing World, *The (Singapore) Straits Times*, 4/2/97

Welsing, Frances Cress, M.D., *The Isis Papers*, Third World Press, Chicago (1991)

Whitmont, Edward C., *The Symbolic Quest: Basic Concepts of Analytical Psychology,* Princeton University Press (1991).

Wilson, Amos, *The Falsification of African Consciousness*, Afrikan World Information Systems, New York (1993)

NEWS PUBLICATIONS

Angier, Natalie, "Do Races Differ? Not Really DNA Shows", New York Times, 8/22/00.

Brooks, Geraldine, Eritrea's Leaders Angle for Sea Change in Nation's Diet to Prove Fish Isn't Foul, *The Wall Street Journal*, 6/2/94

Brown, David, Study: Discrimination May Cause Hypertension in Blacks, *The Washington Post*, 10/24/96

Cashford, Jules and Jones, J.D.F., Death is Outwitted by Gods Reborn in Spring, *Weekend Financial Times*, 4/3/94

Cooke, Kieran, How Malaysia Discarded its Fear of China, *The Financial Times*, 2/10/95

Champy, James, Breathless, And the Race is Hardly Begun, AMA Management Review, January 1995

Dionne, E.J., Jr., *The Washington Post*, 2/9/93

Emecheta, Buchi as quoted in West Blasted for Ugly Image of Africa, by Holtkamp, Rieks, *The Final Call*, date unknown

Financial Times, Weekly Calendar, 7/28/97

Foerstel, Karen, New Black History Unearthed in City, *New York Post*, 8/4/97

Freeman, Dr. Harold P., as quoted by Angier, Natalie, "Do Races Differ? Not Really DNA Shows", New York Times, August 22, 2000.

Hardy, Michael, and Ruff, Jamie C., Wilder Pardons Rape-Case Inmate, *Richmond Times-Dispatch*, date unknown.

James, Frank E., More Blacks Quitting White-Run Firms, *The Wall Street Journal*.

Kaufman Jonathan, Odd Couple: How Omar Green, 27, Became the Point Man and Protégé for a CEO, *The Wall Street Journal*, 7/22/97

Labich, Kenneth, Kissing Off Corporate America, *Fortune*, 2/20/95

McMullen, Larry, *Philadelphia Daily News*, 3/23/81

Packer, William, Symbolism of the Still Life, *Financial Times*, date unknown.

Postgate, John, Religion; Are We Better Off Without It?, *Weekend Financial Times*, June 18-19, 1994

Reich, Robert, Are Consultants Worth Their Weight? *Financial Times*, 5/24/95

Schapiro, Jeff E., and Hardy, Michael, Allen Is Accused of Symbolism Over Substance, *Richmond Times-Dispatch*, 6/6/96

Stevens, William K., Dust and Sea Mud May Link Human Evolution to Climate, *The New York Times,* 12/14/93

Stone Chuck, Naja, OIC and Black Responsibility, *Philadelphia Daily News*, 11/25/80

Street Talk, City Morale Seems Nothing to Cheer About, *STYLE Weekly*, Richmond, VA, 8/5/97

Venter, Dr. Craig J., as quoted by Angier, Natalie, "Do Races Differ? Not Really DNA Shows", New York Times, August 22, 2000.

Williams, Bruce, The Lost Pharoahs of Nubia, *Archaeology Magazine*, Vol. 33, No. 5

Williams, Linda Stress of Adapting to White Society Cited as Major Cause of Hypertension in Blacks, *The Wall Street Journal,* 5/28/86

Winslow, Ron, Blacks Face Higher Risk in Heart Disease, *The Wall Street Journal,* 3/28/96

INDEX